CW00393512

SEEING THROUGH ILLUSIONS

SEEING
THROUGH
ILLUSIONS

RICHARD GREGORY

OXFORD
UNIVERSITY PRESS

OXFORD

UNIVERSITY PRESS

Great Clarendon Street, Oxford OX2 6DP

Oxford University Press is a department of the University of Oxford.
It furthers the University's objective of excellence in research, scholarship,
and education by publishing worldwide in

Oxford New York

Auckland Cape Town Dar es Salaam Hong Kong Karachi
Kuala Lumpur Madrid Melbourne Mexico City Nairobi
New Delhi Shanghai Taipei Toronto

With offices in

Argentina Austria Brazil Chile Czech Republic France Greece
Guatemala Hungary Italy Japan Poland Portugal Singapore
South Korea Switzerland Thailand Turkey Ukraine Vietnam

Oxford is a registered trade mark of Oxford University Press
in the UK and in certain other countries

Published in the United States
by Oxford University Press Inc., New York

© Richard Gregory 2009

The moral rights of the author have been asserted
Database right Oxford University Press (maker)

First published 2009

British Library Cataloguing in Publication Data
Data available

Library of Congress Cataloging in Publication Data
Data available

Typeset by SPI Publisher Services, Pondicherry, India
Printed in Great Britain
on acid-free paper by
CPI Antony Rowe, Chippenham, Wiltshire

ISBN 978-0-19-280285-9

1 3 5 7 9 10 8 6 4 2

ACKNOWLEDGEMENTS

I would like to extend my thanks to the many students and colleagues, especially Dr Priscilla Heard, who have shared the excitement of trying to understand perception, and to the University of Bristol who have extended support and facilities far beyond normal retirement. Most warm thanks to my PA Diana Wilkins for tireless help in making this book and other work possible; to Latha Menon and the Oxford University Press for continuous support and encouragement in this and in other projects. Most particularly I am extremely grateful to the Gatsby Charitable Foundation for supporting my research over many years.

CONTENTS

CONTENTS

PICTURE ACKNOWLEDGEMENTS

CHAPTER 1

PARADIGMS OF PERCEPTION

The truth about truth is elusive;
Is Philosophy merely delusive?
What seems rubbish to you,
May be for me true,
Which leaves everything inconclusive.

Why illusions?

Strange, unusual objects and events inspire questions demanding answers. So science focuses on phenomena. Not only phenomena of the physical world, but also peculiarities of mind. Illusions are strange phenomena of perception that challenge our sense of reality. Though seldom taken seriously by science—as errors are generally nuisances to be avoided rather than phenomena of interest—explaining why illusions occur can reveal how perception works and secrets of brain and mind.

Our aim is to present a variety of illusions, and try to see what they mean for understanding mind and brain. A central theme is that *interpreting* observations and results of experiments is as important as *discovery*. For implications are from interpretations—not directly from phenomena. For example, thunder and lightning have quite different implications when thought of as the wrath of the gods, or moving electrical charges as in a van de Graaff generator. Phenomena must to some degree be explained as having meaning, preferably related to other phenomena. Indeed classifying is important throughout science—for species of plants and animals, for example, and chemical elements and stars—because classifying links phenomena to theories, and gaps reveal questions to be answered. We hope to give meaning to the phenomena of illusions through classifying them by Kinds and Causes.

Our title *Seeing Through Illusions* has two meanings, which flip in the head, like the well-known Duck-Rabbit illusion (Figure 16). 'Seeing through' might refer to an aid to vision, such as a telescope; or very differently, to a warning of being cheated as in 'seeing through a swindle'.

It is impossible to hold both perceptions or both meanings in mind simultaneously. Meanings of words and perceptions of the senses may flip spontaneously or may be selected by context. 'Seeing through a window' has just one familiar meaning, while 'seeing through a project' has another quite different meaning, of continuing until completion. Our title 'seeing through illusions' allows alternative meanings, as illusions evoke a wealth of perceptions and ideas, which we will try to explore.

When the duck-rabbit drawing flips the brain changes its mind, with no change of the picture. Perceptions can flip not only with pictures, but also with normal objects. Then, some perceptions will clearly be different from the object that is seen. This suggests that perceptions are not directly related to objects. This is so, though vision seems vividly 'real' and directly related to things we see. Yet this is, perhaps, the greatest illusion of all. Though seeing feels simple and easy, half the cortex of the human brain is actively involved in reading retinal images—using, for seeing, about 4 per cent of the energy of the food we eat.

Remarkably, it has only been known since early in the seventeenth century that seeing starts with retinal images, the eyes providing neural signals read by the brain as external objects. Visual signals are processed initially in the retina, which is an outgrowth of the brain, by three layers of nerve cells. Then electrical pulses of action potentials pass along the million fibres of the optic nerve to be read by the brain's wonderfully organized structures, using knowledge of objects stored in memory. So the present is seen through knowledge of the past, which may be misleading.

Illusions can result, very differently, from *physiological* errors of signalling or *cognitively* from misleading knowledge, for reading signals from the eyes' images. Although 'physiological' and 'cognitive' illusions have such different causes some appear similar, so may easily be confused. Malfunctioning physiology and misleading knowledge can have surprisingly similar effects; yet their implications for understanding what is going on are very different, so it is important to classify them appropriately.

For medical practice, classifications are clearly important; a diagnosis for a headache that confuses physiological with psychological illness could be lethal. For the science of perception, confusing 'physiological' with 'cognitive' can mislead aims of research and make nonsense of what is discovered. Classifying is really important in science, both theoretical and applied.

Much of science is concerned with analysing phenomena, in depth and detail, but seeing where they fit understanding is equally important. The theories of Galileo and Einstein changed thinking in physics and astronomy by relating familiar phenomena in new ways. Einstein's idea for explaining why small grains of pollen seen in a microscope are continually moving, in a rapid, random dance, created a new science from this trivial-looking observation. By supposing that the pollen grains are buffeted by invisibly small atoms in constant motion, Einstein showed that atoms are more than mathematical concepts, but exist as causally effective objects. From the dance of the pollen Einstein estimated the size of atoms, and introduced the quantum mechanics that has dominated so much of science for a century and still does. This interpretation of already well-known Brownian movement was published by Einstein in 1905 and won him the Nobel Prize. Often, what turn out to be important phenomena looked trivial before they were related to other phenomena with appropriate concepts. Surely, the phenomena of illusions are not exceptions.

As the American philosopher of science Thomas Kuhn said in *The Structure of Scientific Revolutions* (1962), scientists usually accept prevailing working assumptions without spending much time questioning them. This is the basis of what Kuhn called 'normal science'. The principle paradigm for biology is, of course, Darwin's evolution by natural selection, which gives meaning to just about every fact of life. Psychology is unusual, and is not a 'normal' science, as it lacks generally agreed paradigms. There are rival 'schools of thought', with very different assumptions and methods, ranging from introspection to behaviourism.

We have hinted that vision involves optics, physiology, information processing, problem solving, and probability. With these ingredients, we may seek a paradigm to share for seeing how we see, and why we have illusions, though it will not be simple and there will be speculations.

It is an interesting game to challenge alternative paradigms with well-established facts. The rival paradigms can be scored for their ability to incorporate each of the test facts, or phenomena (Gregory 1974). But there is a circularity here, for it is *interpretations* of the facts and phenomena that have implications— but the interpretations depend on the paradigm. This circularity seems central in science, so evidently, science is not as 'objective' as it may seem.

What are perceptions?

The Great Divide for paradigms of perception is whether, for example, vision is *passive reception* of the world of objects or whether it *actively constructs* its versions of reality like a detective building up a case from snippets of evidence. The view taken here is that perception and behaviour developed through evolution from passive responses (which we may call *reception*) to active constructions of full-blown *perceptions*, guesses of what is out there, essentially like predictive hypotheses of science.

Thinking of perceptions as like hypotheses of science, is quite satisfactory for how perceptions are related to the world of objects—indirectly with a lot of guessing—but this tells us nothing about *experience*. For hypotheses of science are not (we assume) conscious. We think of the brain as an incredibly complicated computing machine that creates hypotheses; but this does not help thinking about consciousness, simply because man-made computing machines are not conscious. As the brain is a uniquely conscious machine there is a shortage, indeed an absence, of analogies from machines to *qualia* of sensations in perception. So consciousness is on its own, outside nets of analogies that generally give structure and meaning in science. This lack of functional analogies drives us into philosophy, where the Greek philosophers were at least as wise as we.

A popular account is that perceptions are *pictures in the head.* Does this make sense?

Is the visual brain a picture book?

When we see a tree, is there a tree-like picture in the brain? The trouble with this idea is, it would need something like an eye in the brain to see its pictures. But this internal eye would need another eye to see its pictures—then another eye—and so on forever—an infinite sequence of eyes and pictures without getting anywhere. Although we experience 'mental images' these cannot be pictures in the brain.[1]

There are, however, pictures in the eyes. But they are never seen. The retinal images provide information for seeing, but are not themselves seen. This is rather as a television camera might be used to send signals to a robot's computer, to act on this information though without internal pictures in the robot brain. Components in the computer may represent green leaves, for example; but they will not be leaf-shaped and certainly will not turn green in the spring! Similarly, we should not think of hearing as listening to sounds in the brain. This would start a similar useless infinity of internal sounds and ears.

There are no such sounds and no such pictures, heard or seen in the brain. But if the computer *describes* the camera's picture, by noting which simple features are present, recorded with symbols in some kind of language, this should avoid the infinite regress of internal pictures viewed by internal eyes. Could the brain *represent*, or *describe*, like words in a book? A book needs a reader. But a description is different from an internal picture needing an infinity of eyes and pictures—when the description can be used without further description.

The visual brain does not receive objects, but only bits and pieces of evidence for inferring or guessing what might be out there. The brain creates *descriptions* from simple features received from the senses and represented by the activity of specialized neurons of the brain. Representations may be stored in memory, and indeed perception and memory are closely related.

An important question is: what features are signalled by the eyes and other senses as evidence of external objects? Experiments recording activity of neurons, using fine wires as microelectrodes, have discovered brain circuits 'tuned' to simple features. (Hubel & Weisel 1962). Take the letter **A**. This shape could be represented by three special neural circuits: one responding to the first line sloping up to the right, another to the line sloping to the left, a third to the horizontal between them. It would also have to represent where these are in relation to each other. This is not a difficult task for a computer. Quite simple computers can recognize print, and even handwriting, as for Optical Character Recognition (OCR) in word processors. Such descriptions from the presence of identifying features, do not have the 'infinite regress' problem of brain- or computer-internal pictures.

Words can represent objects, though unlike pictures, they have very different shapes and colours and sizes from whatever it is they are representing. The shape of the word **CAT** is not at all similar to the shape of the animal it represents. And of course words can represent abstract ideas which have no shape, such as 'beauty' or 'truth', 'clever' or 'funny'. This suggests a remarkably interesting idea that occurred to the English philosopher John Locke over three hundred years ago. If the shapes and colours of *words* can be quite different from what they represent, why shouldn't *sensations*, such as red or loud, be quite different from what they represent? Why should the sensation of blue of a summer sky be at all like the colour of sky itself? The sensation might *represent* the sky even though entirely different, as the shape, colour, and size of CAT are very different from the animal the word represents.

John Locke and Sir Isaac Newton in the seventeenth century understood that colours are *created* by brains. They realized that light and objects are not themselves coloured. This still seems surprising. We know now where in the brain this creation of sensations takes place, though how the physical brain produces conscious sensations (*qualia*) is not understood.

If colour and loudness are not in the physical world of objects, and are very different from our experiences, *are all perceptions illusions*? Is it *illusion* that the sky appears blue and thunder sounds loud? Colour and loudness do have physical bases, wavelengths of light and energies of vibrating air, but these physical events are extremely different from sensations.

It is sometimes said that *all* perception is a grand illusion. But this does not help. We may be driven into saying that 'everything is illusion', but this is as pointless as saying 'everything is a dream'. For when applied to everything, the words 'dream' and 'illusion' cease to have meaning. We need contrasts for seeing, and contrasts for describing and thinking. To claim that there is an illusion, there must be some contrasting *non*-illusion. This applies across the board. If every object were red there would be no point in seeing red, or using the word 'red'.

What are illusions?

We may say that *illusions are departures from reality*—but what reality? Appearances are very different from deep realities of physics. If these are taken as reference truths we would have to say that all perceptions are illusions. This is as pointless as saying that perception is a dream.

Illusions are judged with simple common-sense ideas of physics, and measured with kitchen instruments: rulers, clocks, scales, thermometers, and so on. We might define illusions as *deviations from kitchen physics*.

What deviates are the brain's representations of what is out there. A theme of this book is that the brain's representations are *hypotheses*, predictive like the hypotheses of science. Like science, perception bets from available evidence on what is likely to be true—and from what is likely to be true it evaluates the evidence. On this account, we have no certainties.

For both science and perception *phenomena cannot speak for themselves*. Phenomena have to be *interpreted* to have significance. Inferences are not directly from phenomena or data, but from *interpretations*. It seems that science is not as objective as is often claimed.

For perception, there is always guessing and going beyond available evidence. On this view, the closest we ever come to the object world is by somewhat uncertain hypotheses, selected from present evidence and enriched by knowledge from the past. Some of this knowledge is inherited—learned by the statistical processes of natural selection and stored by the genetic code. The rest is brain-learning from individual experience, especially important for humans.

We should look, if briefly, at the evolution of perception. Our evolutionary history is not of 'merely academic' interest, for the past remains in our nervous systems. Ancient behaviour patterns lie deep in our brains, some out of date and no longer appropriate. These may be suppressed and so inactive. When released, as inhibition fails, they may evoke ancient perceptions and behaviour bizarre for present living. As behaviour patterns were laid down through eons of time and not altogether lost, it is important to recognize them as symptoms for understanding neurology and its diseases. The study of behaviour patterns laid down as strata in the nervous system through evolutionary time we may call neuro-archaeology.

The simplest organisms respond fairly predictably to a range of stimuli, with tropisms and reflexes that were appropriate long ago, though may or may not be appropriate now. The 'higher' animals, especially ourselves, are less predictable or lawful than simpler creatures. We are so unlawful that many philosophers and scientists have seen us, or at least our minds, as lying outside science. René Descartes in the seventeenth century famously argued that although our bodies are machines, our minds are beyond any science for explaining. He saw mind and matter as so different they cannot be bridged with concepts or analogies acceptable to science.

This has changed recently, doubtless from familiarity with computers, for computers have many of the strange properties of mind: they don't respond in direct ways to inputs; some can initiate behaviour, as for a chess computer selecting which moves to play; and computers can learn. Some can see, though nothing like as well as us, and in various ways hear and touch and taste and smell. They can calculate much faster and more accurately than we can. Above all, some computers are machines that make decisions from learned rules and knowledge represented in their software. So biological brains are no longer entirely on their own.

Since Charles Babbage's mechanical computer of the 1830s, the idea of machines with minds of their own has become familiar through digital technology. It is indeed remarkable that even simple gear wheels can do 'mental arithmetic', as realized from the middle of the seventeenth century and yet we still speak of *mental* arithmetic. Although the brain is not much like available computers in detail, our familiarity with them has made it easier to accept that minds live in machines—that brains are machines. Yet, computer software and brainy mind still have a spooky, ghostly quality that haunts us and is rather frightening.

What is cognitive perception?

While simple creatures respond quite directly to stimuli, 'higher' animals see and behave in response to guessed *causes* of stimuli. This move from responding to stimuli, to planning behaviour from attributed causes, to anticipated results is, we may say, moving from primitive *reception* to full-blown cognitive *perception*. It is cognitive because perception requires knowledge, knowledge of the world of objects.

This knowledge is *implicit*, to be recognized from experiments on perception and behaviour. Some illusions give evidence for

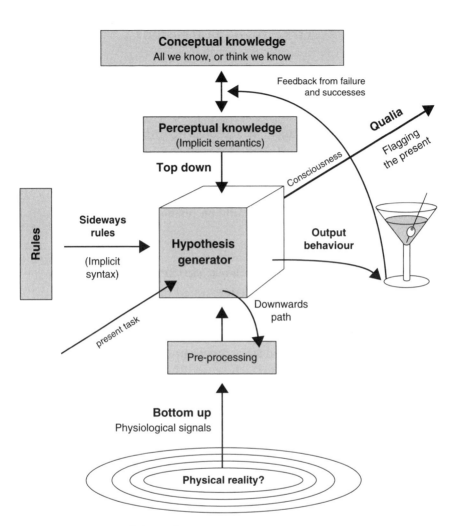

Figure 1. Ins and Outs of Vision.

Figure 1 is a simple conceptual model, rather than an anatomical scheme, for Ins and Outs of Vision. Sensory *signals* are shown as feeding 'upwards' into a Hypothesis Generator creating perceptual hypotheses—perceptions—of what may be out there.

Perceptual *knowledge* working 'downwards' is essential for interpreting, giving meaning, to sensory signals. Perceptual *rules*, such as perspective for seeing depth, are fed in 'sideways', as we may say. Conceptual knowledge is shown as separate from, though linked to, perceptual knowledge. Output *behaviour* can give learning by feedback from errors.

implicit knowledge, when it misleads. The knowledge may be of *particular* objects (such as one's front door key) or general *rules* applying to all objects (such as perspective convergence of lines signalling distance for any object). A diagram might be useful (Figure 1) for showing how this might be organized in the cognitive brain. It will introduce some non-standard terms and, though compatible with currently understood brain anatomy, will be based primarily on phenomena of perception and behaviour.

We may define visual perception as *attributing objects to images*. Attributions are from knowledge, stored from past experience, with associated probabilities. It may be impossible to see anything that has zero probability. A baby inherits some knowledge, giving an essential start to perception.

Bayesian probability

The notion is of prior probabilities modified by present evidence—and conversely reliability of the evidence being judged from the prior probability. This is now formulated with Bayes's theorem. The Reverend Thomas Bayes (1702–61) published little in his lifetime, but he left a now famous manuscript, 'An essay towards solving a problem in the doctrine of chances'. It was found in his papers by his friend Richard Price and published in the *Philosophical Transactions of the Royal Society* in 1763.[2] Ignored or forgotten for 150 years, its ideas have recently become central for economic decisions, and suggestive for how perception works.

The nature of probability remains puzzling and controversial. There are two very different ways of thinking about probability: as ratios of frequencies, and as states of mind. The first is 'objective' and the second is 'subjective', introducing the observer into science. Bayes's theorem is based on subjective probabilities, making beliefs of the observer central. This makes it relevant for indirect, especially constructive theories of perception.

Bayes's theorem gives rules for calculating the likelihood of hypotheses from *prior probabilities* from previous evidence, and from the likelihood of new evidence—the *posterior probability*—being true if the hypothesis is true. The rules are: multiply the prior probability of the hypothesis by the likelihood of the evidence should the hypothesis be true. Take the ratio of these numbers. This gives the odds in favour of the hypothesis. The posterior probability can be used as the prior for another perception, especially for updating a series of perceptions sequentially through time.

It seems that the brain can store several alternative perceptual hypotheses, each with its prior probability. Also, if the Bayesian model is taken literally, the brain can carry out quite complicated algebra without help of written symbols.

Is this how the perceptual brain works? If the brain is analogue, as it seems to be from its slow (compared with electronic components) and richly parallel wiring, it is hard to believe it capable of carrying out the sequential digital calculations necessary for Bayesian inference. Or, can something like Bayesian inference be carried out by analogue processing? Perhaps we should return to visit the cybernetic analogue ideas of fifty years ago, before the power and range of digital computers seduced neuroscience! This is effectively done with interactive neural nets, which are for convenience simulated on digital computers though are analogue in spirit, as they do not follow steps of computations with algorithms. There is significant research potential here.

A major question is how prior probabilities are derived. Are priors from *all* experience? Or is what is learned, selected as likely to be important?[3] This is an empirical question demanding experimental evidence. Phenomena of illusions are suggestive.

The Hollow Face illusion (Figure 19) shows the power of prior probabilities, no doubt from a very large number of faces all being convex. The *stationary moving staircase* (escalator) illusion suggests that priors can be from highly specific learning. The expectation that it is moving makes a stationary escalator quite dangerous. This expectation applies only to normally moving staircases, which are special objects, even for residents of major cities.

This is a special and unusual illusion, but the question of where priors come from applies to well-known and much discussed illusions such as the Ponzo and the Muller-Lyer 'perspective' distortions (Figures 36 and 37). Are parallel lines and right-angular corners especially attractive for perceptual learning? Or, is constancy scaling (if this theory is right) set from the statistics of *all* perceptual experience? The answer is important for theories and practice of perceptual learning, and it is important for experiments using statistics of the real world. I am inclined to believe that we learn what is worth learning and that some of this selection, such as for faces, is innate, being inherited.

Evolution of cognition

How, in their evolution, did nervous systems become cognitive? It may be absurd to suppose that an earthworm is aware of its surroundings, planning its actions from explicit knowledge; though Darwin himself did show how remarkable earthworm behaviour can be. We should ask: What is so very special about the 'higher' animals, including ourselves? Unfortunately we know far too little about perception in animals that cannot speak. For all we have learned through 'objective' experiments using psycho-physics and physiological recordings from nervous systems—which is a great deal—for human beings we learn immeasurably more through language. This is perhaps especially so for illusions, even though we cannot compare our *sensations* with what other people experience.

Our knowledge of illusions in other species is disappointingly small. Do they have the wonderful variety that we experience? We do not know what it is like to be a bat. (Nagel 1974)

A central theme of this book is classifying visual phenomena of illusions, by kinds and causes. This is summarized in a 'Peeriodic Table' (pp. 242). We may start with a list of principle kinds of illusions: **Blindness, Ambiguity, Instability, Distortion, Fiction, Paradox.**

There are many kinds of **Blindness**, from complete and general to partial and selective. Blindnesses can be essential for preventing overloading by irrelevant stimuli or trivial information. **Ambiguities** are rich phenomena of great interest. The word 'ambiguity' is itself ambiguous, for it can mean confounding differences, and very differently, it can mean perceiving differences that are not present. We may call these respectively, 'Confounded Ambiguity' and 'Flipping Ambiguity'.

Instabilities are somewhat similar to Flipping Ambiguities, but deserve a separate category. **Distortions** are the most complex, most controversial, and in some ways the most interesting phenomena of vision. Opinions remain divided on which are due to physiological errors of neural signalling and which to inappropriate scaling of size and distance. The first are 'physiological', the second 'cognitive'.

Perceptions can be **Fictions**, taking off more or less entirely from the object world. They are the basis of much art. No doubt there is some fiction in all perceptions, including observations of science.

Perceptions can be impossible—by being too unlikely or by being **Paradoxical**. Probabilities are important throughout perception. Paradoxes can occur early or late in perceptual processing. The spiral after-effect is seen as expanding (or shrinking) and yet not changing size. The Penrose Triangle, though simple, appears impossible to make in three-dimensional space. The Magritte painting (Plate) is only a stage more impossible than any picture's paradox of three dimensions on a two dimensional surface. Mirror images are impossible, as the same object is seen in two places at the same time, and vision separates from touch. Mirror reversals are remarkably puzzling, perhaps because reflections cannot be touched.

Reception to Perception

A central concept and important distinction is: *'bottom-up' signals* from the senses and *'top-down' knowledge* represented in the brain. Either can produce illusions. It is most important to assign bottom-up and top-down causes appropriately, though not always easy. Misclassifying can be dangerous, as obvious in medical practice, and makes a nonsense of observations and experiments for science. Indeed, classifying phenomena appropriately is as important as discovering them.

We may see evolutionary development in terms of a progression from bottom-up passive responding to stimuli, to active top-down guessing of what is out there. Responses of early organisms to stimuli we may call *'Reception'*, reserving *'Perception'* to 'high-level' cognitive experience, with associated intelligent behaviour. The key here is responding to *attributed* objects and situations, rather than *directly* to stimuli. So, there is evolutionary development from bottom-up responses to top-down knowledge.

Considering the perhaps uniquely human capacity for abstract thinking, we may introduce as a final category 'Conception'. *Reception* ⇒ *Perception* ⇒ *Conception* forms a suggested evolutionary sequence. Evolution may be seen as developing from *Reception* in simple organisms, to knowledge-based cognitive *Perception*; then finally to *Conception* of abstract 'seeing' of thinking.

The earlier responses are to some extent retained in later species; thus we still have rapid reflex responses to ancient dangers. All three capacities—Reception, Perception, and Conception—serve our survival and, most wonderfully, make surviving an exciting adventure full of pleasure as well as pain. We are fortunate to be so late in evolution that we largely escape its life-death horrors. It is most fortunate that we can ask questions, sometimes finding useful and intellectually satisfying answers.

Illusions of *Reception* are primarily physiological distortions of signals from the senses. Illusions of *Perception* include errors of interpreting signals, due to inappropriate knowledge and false assumptions. Here there is no failure of the physiology; but rather, normally functioning processes are *misapplied*, and so inappropriate to the current situation.

This is an important, though often confused distinction. We see this kind of distinction in war. Weapons may *malfunction*, as when a gun misfires, or they may fire *inappropriately* by poor strategy. These are different much as physiological functions and cognitive processes are different—though the same objects, indeed the same atoms, serve physiology and cognition simultaneously. Cognition is not in a 'balloon' above the brain. It is how physiological resources are applied, for perception and thinking and intelligent behaviour. As the resources are quite frequently misapplied, cognition is far from infallible, as we shall see from some kinds of illusions and errors of thinking.

Deception is an ever-present theme, applying to Reception, Perception, and Conception. All are subject to various kinds of illusions, which may be evoked by enemies, as secret weapons hidden within the victim.

The emphasis here is on *phenomena of vision*, and what they can tell us of the nature of perception. This might perhaps be useful for artists, who play upon our perceptions rather as violinists play upon the strings of their instruments. As science has learned a great deal about perception from artists, I hope this book may in a small way repay science's debt to artists. Understanding of science may extend the arts, as art extends science. An issue here is the possibility, which is sometimes feared, that explicit understanding may inhibit artistic creativity.

Does understanding have such a downside? I doubt it. Violinists need to know a great deal, at least implicitly, about the physical possibilities of the strings and resonances of their instruments. But how far should this be explicit? Would an appreciation of Fourier analysis and synthesis of sound help musicians, or just possibly be a hindrance to them? Does an understanding of how the lens of the eye focuses light, and of the physical basis of colours, help the painter? Is it useful for artists to think of *perceptions* as evolved from primitive *reception*, or of hypotheses obeying Bayesian rules of probability inference? I rather think the answer is 'yes'.

Phenomena cannot speak for themselves

An eclipse of the sun is dramatic and wonderful - but what do we see? Early explanations invoked predictions and threats of the gods. Now eclipses evoke movements of the solar system—the earth going round the sun and the moon going round the earth nearly in the same plane, with critical sizes and distances, all obeying Newtonian laws. This mental model gives the eclipse phenomena very different meaning, with very different implications.

We *see* phenomena as we *understand* them by the current model in mind. Conversely phenomena can suggest and test mental models. Without a model, we are blind with agnosia. The point here is that phenomena of illusions may suggest and test mental models for seeing how we see.

The most mysterious output is consciousness. Some, though not all, perceptions are associated with *qualia*—of red, bright, black, and so on: sensations in sensory experience. How qualia are generated by the brain is deeply mysterious. But perhaps we should not be worried that qualia of sensation and the physiological processes generating them are so different. It is not unusual for combinations of causes to be very different from the result. For example, oxygen and hydrogen combine to produce the very different properties of water. Assembling a model from a Meccano kit, makes say a working model clock, with quite different properties from the bits of metal in the box. And the mechanism of a clock is extremely different from the (mysterious) time it records.

What, if anything, do qualia do? Given evolution and natural selection, we should expect consciousness to have some survival-enhancing function. Is it possible that qualia of consciousness serve to *flag the present moment*? Perception is based on ancient, innate, and on more recent learned knowledge from the past, with present information from the senses for real-time behaviour. Possibly qualia flag the present, to keep the present separate from confusion with knowledge from the past. It matters that a traffic light is red or green *now*, though it is from the past that we have learned why it matters, and the pay-off is in the future. There are rare examples of people with exceptional memories who do confuse the past with the present, notably Mr S. described by the Russian neurologist Alexander Luria (1969). He would confuse the memory of his alarm clock with seeing it, and fail to get up in the morning. Confusing past with present is dangerous. There is normally something special, especially vivid, in qualia from the present. Is this a reason for consciousness?

As we have said (p. 4) there is a circularity (or perhaps tennis-like to and fro) between phenomena and how they are interpreted or explained. The reader might like to enter this game of how science works, by considering these phenomena of illusions and the explanations on offer. This account is not engraved on stone, but might for the moment be a useful doodle in the sand.

Notes

1. This argument (though for hearing) was proposed by the Greek philosopher Theophrastus (c.372–286 BCE) when criticizing Empedocles for saying that perceptions are copies: 'It is strange of him (Empedocles) to imagine that he has explained how creatures hear, when he has ascribed the process to internal sounds, and assumed that the ear produces a sound within, like a bell. By means of this internal sound we might hear sounds without, but how should we hear this internal sound itself? The old problem would still confront us.

2. *Philosophical Transactions of the Royal Society* LIII (1763), 370–418. Reprinted in *Biometrica* 45 (1958): 296–315.

3. For example, faces attract the attention of young babies, and identities of their carers are soon learned.

CHAPTER 2

NEURO-
ARCHAEOLOGY

Although the theory of evolution is now almost universally accepted, puzzles remain that intrigue experts and stimulate research in all areas of biology and the study of mind. For a long time the origins of our species *homo sapiens* seemed to be suspiciously special—derived from only one line of ancestors—which would make it unique and outside Darwin's paradigm. But recently alternative possible early ancestors living around the same time have been identified from fossils found in various regions in Africa. So our origins are no longer seen as special, but as for other species, to have evolved from a branching tree of candidates. Natural selection may be seen as the Great Intelligence that designed all living things, though apparently without intention or purpose. This has upset some people, and no doubt it puts the onus on us to create intentions and purposes giving meaning to our lives.

Darwin's theory has significant implications throughout the whole of biology, including cognitive psychology. How much knowledge is *inherited* from successes and failures of ancestral battles? How much is *learned* by individual experience? Inheritance from past species certainly occurs for anatomy, and innate implicit knowledge clearly dominates simpler animals; dramatically so for ants and bees, or consider the astonishing behaviour of migrating and nest-building birds. So it would be odd if past skills of behaviour and perception were not passed on to us, as babies, modified by learning as we become adult.

It can be useful to use the word '*knowledge*' broadly—implicit knowledge—to include reflexes and behaviour patterns, and even complex social behaviour. We see with ancestral eyes and brains, and behave appropriately to lost worlds; though of course ancient worlds were not entirely different from ours. Inherited anatomy cannot be entirely separate from behaviour, as all animals use their anatomical forms as tools and weapons closely linked to behaviour. Our technologies, from the earliest wooden and flint tools, extend our anatomy to accomplish superhuman tasks such as flying faster than the speed of sound, and producing and reading books. Minds are inconceivable without functioning bodies and tools of technology transform our bodies.

Primitive perception (or rather 'reception') is largely innate. Sophisticated perception is based on knowledge of likely causes of stimuli—hypotheses of what may be out there. Some of our behaviour is from primitive reception, as when we blink at a sudden noise without knowing what causes it, because for millions of years bangs have accompanied damage to eyes. Early brains lacked ability to seek the danger behind the bang, so the bang itself had to be sufficient to trigger behaviour.

The genetic code learned that bangs are bad news for eyes. With our knowledge, we can do more to save our sight. We can avoid eye-dangerous situations and invent protections, such as safety goggles, and even with our science-based knowledge mend damaged eyes. This is a long way from reflex blinking.

Although implicit innate knowledge is relatively minor in us, babies only a few hours old will respond to faces, spending more time looking at a face-like drawing than a jumbled face. Babies are born with sufficient implicit knowledge to see faces as important—and they then learn which faces are special.

Some things are far easier to learn than others. Minimal innate knowledge can serve to direct attention for individual learning. As human babies are protected for so long, they have time to extend their inherited gene-knowledge with exploratory experience. Yet, some gene-knowledge remains. Babies like sweet and avoid sour tastes, as sugar was in short supply and sour was associated with poison. Adults still like sweets but learn moderation. It takes hard-won individual brain-knowledge to appreciate a glass of bitter beer.

Present understanding of these issues has been won for us by many talented individuals, some of whom are described below.

Jean-Baptiste Lamarck: is brain-knowledge inherited?

The French naturalist, Chevalier Jean Baptiste Pierre Antoine de Monet Lamarck (1744–1829) was an early evolutionist, recognizing before Darwin that life evolves.[1] He believed that individuals' life experiences can be inherited by their offspring. Darwin was not sure that he was wrong, but it is now established, beyond reasonable doubt, that everything learned by an individual is lost at death.[2] It seems tragic that all we learn in our lives dies with us. It is this that makes rituals, legends, and books so important, though innate knowledge may be millions of years out of date. We need brain-learning to counter out-of-date, inappropriate gene-knowledge, such as irrational fears. But where there is no inherited knowledge we lack immediately available skills and so are vulnerable. Driving above the speed limit with one hand, while telephoning and eating an orange with the other, may feel safe as driving is biologically recent, but it is actually more dangerous than snakes.

John Hughlings Jackson: 'archaeological' layers of brain functions

The great neurologist John Hughlings Jackson (1835–1911) was a considerable philosopher, with important ideas on anatomy and functions of the brain. He thought of them as being, we might say, *archaeologically* layered, as a result of how they were formed through many millions of years of evolution. His key idea was that many 'higher' functions suppress or inhibit older 'lower' functions, which have become obsolete and a hindrance.

In brain damage, including degeneration with ageing, normal inhibitions may be lost. Then ancient, normally suppressed functions emerge as bizarre, though in these terms understandable, clinical symptoms—as the rejected past rises up to haunt the present. This is a unifying idea of great importance for neurology, and for appreciating how the brain is organized from its evolution.[3]

Hughlings Jackson acknowledged his intellectual debt to the polymath Herbert Spencer (1820–1903), who was also an advocate of evolutionary biology before Darwin. One might, indeed, say that ideas in the history of science get inhibited and may later surface, rather like the evolution of brain mechanisms. Jackson said that evolution is from the most organized to the least organized, from the most simple to the most complex, and from the most automatic to the most voluntary. The highest brain centres he calls 'organs of the mind'.

Hughlings Jackson recognized that local brain damage does not produce symptoms directly related to the damage. Rather, local damage releases activity from other regions, and it is this activity that may be inappropriate. He said of nervous disease, that disease does not *cause* the symptoms of insanity:

> A man suffering from local softening of the brain has that defect of speech that consists in uttering wrong words.... No one objects to the clinical statement that softening 'is the cause' of the defect of speech. But strictly speaking it is simply impossible that softening of the brain can cause any wrong utterances; for softened brain is no brain; ... the wrong utterances occur during activity of parts *not* softened but healthy... The positive manifestations are indirectly caused, or rather are 'permitted'.[4]

Jackson described the hierarchy of the brain as organized with three levels, functioning from the lowest to the highest centres, saying:

> The doctrine of evolution implies the passage from the most organised to the least organised, or, in other terms, from the most general to the most special. Roughly, we may say that there is gradual 'adding on' of the more and more special, a continual adding on of new organisations. But this 'adding on' is at the same time a 'keeping down'.

As we have said, what emerges when the 'keeping down' processes fail may be what are now bizarre behaviours or bizarre perceptions.

Ernst Haeckel: recapitulation of evolution

A feature of evolution is that its arrow through time does not generally reverse. Moreover there are seldom entirely new structures. Rather, existing structures take on new and sometimes very different functions. These demand modifications that occur only slowly, so we live in the present with out-of-date structures and knowledge. Something of this is explicit in comparative embryology. This was the idea of the controversial German zoologist Ernst Haeckel (1834–1919), who proposed that the life history of the individual is a recapitulation of the journey of evolution. He expressed this as *ontology recapitulates phylogeny*, ontology being the origin and development of individuals, and phylogeny being the origin and development of species. This is one of the most famous, though also most criticized, statements in the history of biology. Haeckel has a mixed reputation as a philosopher and his ideas are often dismissed; but surely his ontogeny recapitulating phylogeny almost *must* happen, on the Darwinian paradigm, though of course evidence is needed to develop and check the idea. Haeckel saw that this might come from comparisons of development of embryos of various species. He pointed out that ancient characteristics are present in early stages of development of embryos of later species. He produced a famous series of drawings of developing embryos of various species, showing such remarkable similarity at early stages that they are hard to tell apart, though becoming very different with further development (Figure 2). How much he 'improved' his drawings to illustrate the idea remains controversial.

Charles Darwin himself said in *The Origin of Species*: 'Embryology rises greatly in interest when we look at the embryo as a picture, more or less obscured, of the progenitor, either in its adult or larval state, of all the members of the same great class.' A recent authoritative text by the embryologist Lewis Wolpert does not dismiss this, asking: 'Why, for example, do all vertebrate embryos pass through an apparently fish-like phylotypic stage that has structures resembling gill slits?' The answer given is:[5]

> If two groups of animals that differ greatly in their adult structures and habits (such as fishes and mammals) pass through a very similar embryonic stage, this indicates that they are descended from a common ancestor and in evolutionary terms are closely related. Thus an embryo's development reflects the

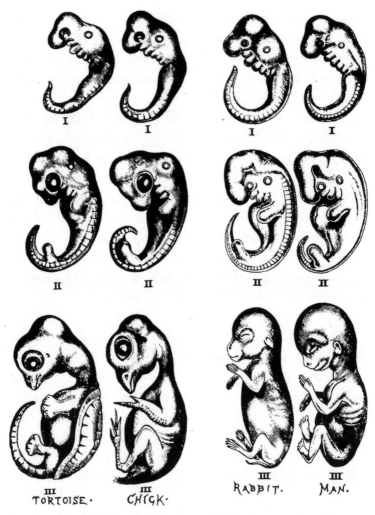

Figure 2. Haeckel's drawings of embryos of various species. At early stages of development they are so similar they are hard to identify.

evolutionary history of its ancestors. Structures found in a particular embryonic stage have become modified during evolution into different forms in the different groups.[6]

It seems hard to dismiss Haeckel's claim completely. Our past lives on in our body, brain, and mind, though we can do some editing and add new chapters.

Arnold Gesell: the embryology of behaviour

What of our individual development? Human behaviour starts at about the fifth week of development of the embryo, this first behaviour being innate. The pioneer of these studies was Arnold Gesell, especially in his *The Embryology of Behaviour* (1945). Gesell essentially follows Haeckel, saying (p. xiii): 'In the biological perspective, the newborn infant is an extreme ancient for he has already traversed most of the stages of his long, racial evolution' (Figure 3).

Gesell's chapter 5, 'The Archaic Motor System', is a good starting point for seeing the 'archeological' time-layers of muscles and their functions. We learn that the oldest muscles are for posture, posture being the basis of all behaviour. Among the oldest are the muscles of the trunk and pelvic girdle, the broad flat overlying muscles being more recent. Ancient, also, are the six extra-ocular muscles of the eyes, going back to lamprey and hagfish. As posture changed over millions of years, from horizontal to the modern human vertical, so major muscles and their neural organization changed to

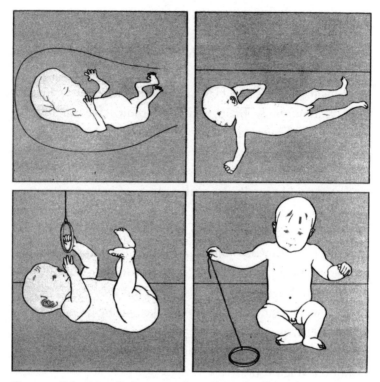

Figure 3. Behaviour of a human embryo. From Gesell (1945).

accommodate the new posture—with greatly revised strategies for moving around and performing new skills.[7]

The development of skills is seen in terms of innate ontology as well as individual learning. Thus: 'Complicated action patterns whose components were ontogenetically and physiologically developed over long reaches of time are telescoped into a single moment of behaviour.'[8] Relating posture to behaviour, Gesell cites the classical studies of swimming behaviour and responses to touch stimuli of salamanders by G. E. Coghill, which distinguished innate development from learning and also from maturation—which may require active behaviour to develop, though it is not learning. These are beautiful experiments.[9]

Features of neurological abnormalities or diseases may be *returns to ancient behaviour patterns*. Is it these that we see in cerebral palsy, in Down's syndrome? The implication, as seen by Hughlings Jackson, is that to understand what is happening with neurological problems we should trace back the phylogeny, to find the individually upset ontology.

Living with out-of-date inherited knowledge

A clear, well-known example of an out-of-date reflex is the Babinski 'sign'. Upon touch to the side of the foot of a baby, the big toe sticks up and the other toes extend and fan out. This is seen as pre-human behaviour for living in trees. Describing human foetal toes and fingers, Gesell says:

> During sleep the fluctuating tonus permits variable lackadaisical or limp posturing. When the tonus is stronger, fingers and toes alike react with patterned fanning to a sudden stimulus. A mild Babinski response suggests an attempt to grasp an object; an exaggerated response suggests repulsion and release. The mobility of the great toe and the adjacent cleft recalls arboreal antecedents, when the feet as well as the hands were nimble and prehensile.

HAND AND FOOT: FETAL-INFANCY

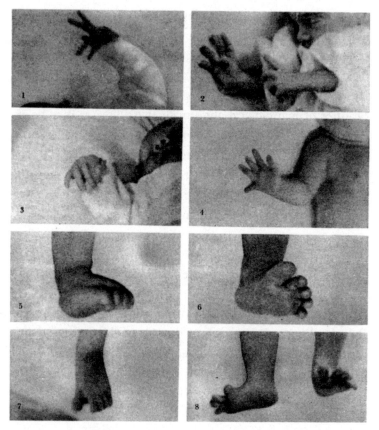

Figure 4. Foetal Babinski reflex. Gesell, *Embryology of Behaviour* (1946).

This reflex was appropriate for monkeys and apes for the toes to grip branches of trees, but became inappropriate for later walking on the ground. The Babinski reflex is normally lost at around 18 months, becoming inhibited. But we live with this out-of-date reflex that remains present in our nervous system but is lying dormant. In some neurological diseases this pre-human reflex awakes, giving the Babinski sign of neural disease, as inhibition from the cortex or spinal cord fails.

It seems that many other infant behaviours, such as sucking, remain dormant but inhibited, sometimes re-appearing many years later with neurological problems. In senility, behaviour patterns inhibited through evolution can emerge in reverse sequence.

In the first year or so of human life, there is a sequence of reflexes allowing the growing baby to support its head, then crawl, then stand and walk. There is a primary reflex, the Asymmetrical Tonic Neck Reflex, which aids the birth process. This appears at about 18 weeks in utero, and is normally inhibited at about six months of life. It helps to develop eye-hand co-ordination as the arm is flung out with head rotation. But if it is not inhibited, as usual at around six months, normal crawling is impossible.

In general, later developments may be upset or be impossible by failed inhibitions of reflexes that, though useful at early stages of development, become inappropriate and even disastrous for later behaviour. Thus, when the infant's life-saving Startle Reflex remains, the adult may respond violently to any sudden noise, as in shellshock, which is disabling.[10]

The very early environment may be important, as highlighted by neonatal development of pre-term babies. What is the optimal stimulation for pre-term babies? Normally, the mother's 'intuitive' touching and light stroking may be relied upon. But for premature babies in an incubator there is possible damage; absence of interaction may also be harmful. Recent research on this topic has practical and theoretical interest.[11]

Evolutionary psychology

Darwin saw natural selection as creating and molding mind. This has recently been stated by evolutionary psychologists John Tooby and Leda Cosmides:[12]

Darwin took [a] radical step toward uniting the mental and physical worlds, by showing how the mental world—whatever it might be composed of—arguably owed its complex organisation to the same process of natural selection that explained the physical organization of living things. Psychology became united with the biological and hence evolutionary science.

Darwin discusses this conception of the origin of mind in many places in his Notebooks and throughout his great book *The Emotions in Man and Animals* (1873), which remains delightful reading today.[13] It is frequently suggested that the human mind, and how we behave in groups, is formed from the evolution of animal behaviour and perception. This is especially credited to the remarkable scholar E. O. Wilson.[14] These ideas are now attracting a great deal of interest in psychology, though most of the evidence has come from animal behaviour, which is hard to interpret for humans as we live in such structured 'artificial' societies. How far have we escaped our biological origins?

According to evolutionary psychology, we live animal lives in human form. The remarkable thing is, we can write and talk about it. We can generally overcome socially dangerous inherited behaviour, though sometimes we are overturned, riding storms of ancient seas.

There are very large inherited species differences of behaviour and perceptual systems. Even the number of eyes is not constant, and inherited behaviour has astonishing variety, even for mammals. But what interests us here is the innate structure of the human mind. Evidence from other species is suggestive, though indirect and hard to interpret. What is the available human evidence for believing that our behaviour and perception are controlled by inheritance from the past, from long before human history? Archaeological evidence is important but sketchy, and too recent, but we may look at our 'living fossil' behaviour and perception.

We do inherit fears and aversions that match dangers of early human life: fear of falling, of snakes, of spiders, of dark closed places, of sudden sounds. There are common and widespread, indeed universal across races. One does have to be careful, though, that such widely shared fears are not due to common childhood experiences, and so learned rather than inherited. But these dangers were far more common thousands of year ago than now, and there is conspicuous lack of fear of *recent* dangers. So children have to be guarded as their innate fears tend not to apply now, and new dangers must be learned before they produce disaster.

What is inherited?

Especially suggestive inherited preferences are gender characteristics of female fertility and male reliability. A primary female attraction is youth, presumably because babies are most frequently born to women aged 17–25, with rapid decline into the 40s. Presumably, men remain attractive for longer because they remain potent, and can continue to protect and support into early old age.[15]

Both sexes show many features we find innately attractive. Women are the more choosy. Universally preferred are symmetrical faces, symmetry being associated with youth and good health, and also indicating absence of genetic 'noise'.

Women's complexion and colour are important signs of health, associated with child rearing. There are marked female body-shape preferences for males, especially the waist-hip-ratio (WHR). Preferred body size varies with different cultures, but universal maximal attraction is a WHR of about 0.7. Looks are more important in women than men; women rate personality characteristics, such as confidence and dominance, as more important than looks. Wealth, generosity, and reliability are rated highly.

It has been shown that in America, professional qualifications are important as attractions. Doctors and professors do well. This raises the general question: What, exactly, is inherited from the human past? Although preferred body shapes might be inherited, from ancient correlation with female fertility and male broad shoulders for hunting prowess, it is absurd to suppose that a PhD is the same. A PhD represents a modern indication of success, and it is attraction to success that is inherited. What exactly is inherited is, surely, a key kind of question to ask of evolutionary psychology. Take aggression: does aggression have to include cruelty? Or does aggression *against* cruelty also come from inheritance? Surely this is an important question, as its answer reflects how innate behaviour and perception can be steered, by education and example, to socially commendable ends.

The more there is such flexibility the better, especially when present needs are different from the original conditions. But this flexibility must make it harder to find clear examples of genetically determined behaviour, especially for discovering just what is inherited and what learned.

It is reasonable to suppose that flowers and trees and warm weather appeal because these were important over a long period. But periods of danger and suffering may have been important too, to avoid indolence and promote quick thinking and planning. Also, what is inherited may be the facility to learn skills.

Language

Since the extraordinarily influential work and ideas of Noam Chomsky, the strongest claim of genetic inheritances of mind has been for language.[16] The present strongest claimer is Steven

Pinker. Writing with charm and authority, Pinker describes the power of language in these terms:

> As you are reading these words, you are taking part in one of the wonders of the natural world. For you and I belong to a species with a remarkable ability: we can shape events in each other's brains with exquisite precision. I am not referring to telepathy. That ability is language. Simply by making noises with our mouths, we can reliably cause precise new combinations of ideas to arise in each other's minds. The ability comes so naturally that we are apt to forget what a miracle it is.[17]

How far the structure of language is innate remains controversial after years of intensive research. The notion seems initially implausible because there are many very different languages. Chomsky's insight was his Deep Structure—that there is a common shared structure underlying all natural languages. Indeed, this idea illustrates the difficulty of knowing just what is genetically coded and inherited as innate knowledge. It is obviously not the words, as these are very different in various languages, and grammars also have marked differences. Chomsky's Deep Structure as underlying all the various grammars is a clever idea. It can only be evaluated by his fellow experts. There seems now, however, to be something of a falling back from Chomsky's position.

Pinker points out apes have no language at all equivalent to ours, which is a surprising gap that needs explaining. His explanation is that living apes are not direct descendants. There is a time-gap, of ten million years, to the common ancestor. This leaves time for our brain mechanisms, and vocalization for human language, to have developed in their own ways.

To make a perhaps naive point, it is often possible to understand a thoroughly ungrammatical sentence, or a sentence with no obvious grammatical structure. This is so for expletives—yet the meaning is clear, especially in a shared situation. 'Good God!' has very different though clear meanings, as in a church or when something extraordinary has happened. Of course tone of voice is effective. But grammar is undoubtedly essential for expressing complicated thoughts. If we want to say anything at all complicated grammatical structure is essential. For example: 'Could you check this reference now and compare it with the first edition before you ask Smith's advice?' But also a great deal of implicit knowledge is involved. Thus, 'Look me up sometime and we will look up the reference' makes surprising sense.

Chomsky's theory is not unlike the notion of perceptions as being hypotheses, constructed by following rules and relying on (innate and learned) knowledge. The issue is the ratio of innate to learned knowledge, for perception and for language.

Innate knowledge was itself originally learned by natural selection, though what the natural selection pressures were for Chomsky's Deep Structure of grammar may not be at all clear. If it developed independently several times, there is certainly a question to answer. I don't know the answer, or where to look for it. Conceivably, language structure derived from pre-linguistic perceptual classifications of objects and actions. One can see nouns and verbs in this way. But surely this leaves mysterious the 'exquisite precision' of language.

Perhaps the point is that we can introspect on language structures and rules—we can, as it were, feel whether a sentence is well formed or grammatical even without knowing rules of grammar explicitly. We feel that, 'She should have knowed better' is wrong, even though we may not be able to say why it is wrong. Children make this kind of mistake with past tenses, as their rules are rather special and modify earlier rules. But we cannot see rules of perception. They have to be discovered by experiments.

It is not obvious why 'Impossible Objects' look impossible, or why distortion illusions such as the Muller-Lyer are related to seeing depth. Conceivably, rules of perception are as rich as rules of language, though not yet as fully recognized.

It is interesting that word processors can warn of grammatical errors and are remarkably good at it. This means that although intuited originally, they have been formulated into explicit computer programs, which work consistently whatever the subject matter of the writing. There is no such complete computer parsing for pictures, though this is an active research enterprise, and has been for forty years. Computers were programmed to analyse and generate impossible pictures as early as late 1960s, with analogy to generative grammars envisaged by Chomsky.[18]

Seeing the past

This Jacksonian 'archaeological' approach will no doubt have even greater clinical possibilities now with the decoding of the human genome. We may need to know the gene sequences of our ancestors, as well as detailed comparative anatomy, to carry out this programme and apply the results effectively. How far will it go? This evokes science fiction, but we may think that as we inherit ancient perceptual knowledge it may be possible to tap into past life forms—even perhaps to discover the sounds and colours of extinct dinosaurs, from innate present responses of living creatures whose ancestors knew them. Could gene sequences, and inherited responses, reveal lost minds? There is no obvious limit to what might remain in the genetic code we inherit.

Doing and seeing

There is good evidence that human vision is both ancient and modern, with their own 'streams' of processing, both emanating from the primary visual area V1 at the back of the brain. There is a *ventral* stream in the inferior temporal cortex, and a *dorsal* stream in the posterior parietal cortex, which is associated with memory. It was originally thought that the dorsal stream is concerned with *where* things are and the ventral stream with *what* they are. It now seems that the distinction is between immediate action and conscious seeing. It seems that only the seeing ventral system is conscious.

Evidence for two cortical streams comes from brain anatomy, and magnetic resonance scanning with functional differences showing up in rare cases of selective brain damage. David Milner and Mel Goodale found that a patient, MM, could use her hands for skilled tasks, such as posting a letter through a narrow slot of various orientations, yet she could not consciously see the letter or the slot. Her vision worked for (rapid) action but not for conscious seeing.

Such clinical evidence is suggestive, but there is always concern that the brain is not normal. Is there evidence of such a separation of behaviour from seeing in normal subjects? Evidence has come from illusions. There are many well-known illusions of distortion (as we shall see and discuss in considerable detail), but here they are used as experimental tools for teasing out differences of seeing and doing—by finding out whether the *visual* illusions affect touch *behaviour*. The evidence is that there can be visual distortions of size though the fingers grasp the visually distorted object normally. As the distortion is in vision but not touch behaviour, they must be associated with different neural systems.[19]

These distortions are small, only a few millimetres, so the experiments are hard to do and are not always confirmed. We have found separation between rapid touching of targets and visual experience of them with a much larger and very robust illusion—the Hollow Face. This is a hollow mask, which is seen as a normal nose-sticking-out face, simply because a hollow face is so unlikely. Subjects touch targets on the hollow mask correctly, though they see them nearer on the illusory normal-looking face. It is quite surprising, as one's hand touches, say, the cheek of the hollow mask, with a rapid flick, though it appears nearer as a convex face. So touch and vision separate quite dramatically. Other experiments have involved touching the circle of the Ebbinghaus (or Titchener) illusion, which appears larger when surrounded by small circles.

The notion of an ancient visual system for rapid action and a more recent system for cognitive planned behaviour, with consciousness, makes evolutionary sense.

Notes

1. Lamarck gives his theory of evolution—denying that species are fixed—in *Philosophie Zoologique* (1809).
2. Of course, humans transmit knowledge through the generations with books and artifacts of many kinds. This cultural transmission of knowledge makes humans a unique species.
3. Hughling Jackson's papers are not easy to read, and he does not always seem to be consistent; but he had insights that illuminate present thinking. He acknowledged an intellectual debt to Herbert Spencer (1820–1903), for thinking along these evolutionary lines, especially Spencer's vast *Principles of Psychology* (1855) which is a daunting undertaking to read. See M. Critchley and E. Critchley, *John Hughlings Jackson: Father of English Neurology.* (Oxford: Oxford University Press, 1998).
4. This is quoted by Critchley and Critchley (1998: 56). It is surely a warning, now, for conceptual care needed for localizing functions from brain imaging. A further ambiguity is that locally increased metabolic rate may be a rise of inhibition, rather than activation.
5. Lewis Wolpert, *Principles of Development* (Oxford: Oxford University Press, 1998), 445.

6. This continues: 'Another example is the branchial arches and gill slits that are present in all vertebrate embryos, including humans. These are not the relics of the gill arches and gill slits of an adult fish-like ancestor, but of structures that would have been present in the embryo of the fish-like ancestor. During evolution, the branchial arches have given rise both to the gills of the primitive jawless fishes and, in a later modification, to jaws. When the ancestor of land vertebrates left the sea, gills were no longer required, but the embryonic structures that gave rise to them persisted.'

7. G. E. Coghill (1914–36), 'Correlated anatomical and physiological studies of the growth of the nervous system of Amphibia', *Journal of Comparative Neurology*, parts I–XII.; Critchley and Critchley (1998); Arnold Gesell, *The Embryology of Behaviour: The Beginnings of the Human Mind* (New York: Harper, 1945); S. Goddard, *A Teacher's Window into the Child's Mind: A Non-Invasive Approach to Learning and Behaviour Problems* (Eugene, OR: Fern Hill Press, 1995); R. Magnus (1925), 'Animal posture' (Croonian Lecture), *Proceedings of the Royal Society B* 98: 339–53; Wolpert, Lewis, *Principles of Development* (Oxford: Oxford University Press, 1998).

8. Gesell (1945: 52).

9. Gesell quotes a less well-known study on ontological mammalian posture and behaviour, by Magnus (1925):

Suppose a cat standing in the middle of the room, and a mouse is running on its right side along the wall. The optic and acoustic stimuli act on telereceptors of the cat's head, and make it turn the heavy head to the right. By this the centre of gravity of the fore part of the body is displaced to the right. At the same time tonic neck reflexes are evoked, by which the vertebral column is curved and the right fore limb strongly extended so that it carries the weight of the body alone and prevents it from falling. The left fore limb has nothing to carry, and in harmony therewith this limb relaxes under the influence of the tonic neck reflex. At the same time the distribution of excitability in the motor centres of the spinal cord is rearranged by turning of the neck, so that . . . the limb which has no static function will always make the first step. In this way . . . the cat is focused towards the mouse and made ready for movement. The only thing the cat

48

has to do is to jump or not to jump: all other things have been prepared beforehand reflexly under the influence of the mouse, which will be the object of the resulting jump.

Gesell comments: 'Magnus demonstrated the presence of these reflexes in idiots and in patients suffering from extrapyramidal tract lesions and erroneously came to the conclusion that in man it is a pathological phenomenon.' But Gesell showed—and surely this is important—that, 'it is a normal characteristic of foetal and early post-foetal human behaviour. It occurs in classic form as early as the 28th foetal week.'

10. There is a school of practising therapists who provide special exercises for giving the nervous system 'a second chance' of inhibiting aberrant reflexes. This was started by Peter Blythe, in 1969, who founded the Institute for Neuro-physiological Psychology, in 1975 in Sweden. This work is described by Sally Goddard (1995). Shouldn't we, as discussed by Sally Goddard, consider this approach for mental problems such as autism? Aberrant reflexes may delay or prevent normal mental development. Possibly there is an effective return to earlier less 'social' brain organization. It is suggestive that during the slow, dreadful progress of Alzheimer's early reflexes reappear, in reversed chronological order.

11. Several studies are described in Elvedina N. Adamson-Macedo, *The Psychology of Pre-term Neonates* (Heidelberg: Mates Verlog, 2002).

12. J. Tooby and L. Cosmides, 'Psychological foundations of culture', in J. Barkow, L. Cosmides, and J. Tooby (eds), *The Adapted Mind* (Oxford: Oxford University Press, 1992), 20.

13. Charles Darwin, *The Expression of the Emotions and Man and Animals* (London: John Murray, 1873). Reprinted University of Chicago Press (1965). For current views: Paul Ekman, *Darwin and Facial Expression: A Century of Research in Review* (New York: Academic Press, 1973). Darwin's account has stood remarkably firm.

14. E. O. Wilson is the world authority on ants. His *Sociobiology: A New Synthesis* (Harvard University Press, 1975), caused a furore when it appeared, and this has hardly died away. A highly readable account of

Evolutionary Psychology, especially sexual selection, is Matt Ridley, *The Red Queen* (Harmondsworth: Penguin, 1993).

15. An excellent text, giving full references, is: David M. Buss, *Evolutionary Psychology (Boston: Allyn and Bacon,* 1999).

16. N. Chomsky, *Syntactic Structures* (The Hague: Mouton, 1957); N. Chomsky, *Rules and Representations* (New York. Columbia University Press, 1980).

17. Steven Pinker, *The Language Instinct* (London: Allen Lane, The Penguin Press, 1994), 15.

18. D. A. Huffman, 'Decision criteria for a class of "impossible" objects', *Proceedings of the First Hawaii International Conference on System Sciences* (Honolulu, 1968); D. A. Huffman, 'Impossible objects as nonsense sentences', *Machine Intelligence 6, ed.* Bernard Meltzer and Donald Michie (Edinburgh: Edinburgh University Press, 1971).

19. The two visual streams idea was suggested by L. G. Ungerleider and M. Mishkinkin (1982), and developed by David Milner and Mel Goodale (1995), with initial evidence from selective brain damage. Very rarely, one of the systems is lost. See A. D. Milner and M. A. Goodale, *The Visual Brain in Action* (Oxford: Oxford University Press, 1995); M. Jeanerod, *The Cognitive Neuroscience of Action* (Oxford: Blackwell, 1997); L. G. Ungerleider and M. Mishkin, 'Two cortical visual systems', in D. J. Ingle, M. A. Goodale, and R. J. W. Mansfield (eds), *Analysis of Visual Behaviour* (Cambridge, MA: MIT Press, 1952), 549–86.

CHAPTER 3

FIRST LIGHT

First Light is the astronomers' celebration of a new telescope as it sees the universe for the first time—a giant glass eye feeding the astronomer's brain with images of unearthly objects, sometimes from the distant past, before life on earth began.

First Light of living eyes was half a billion years ago, on an earth very different from ours. Like all the best journeys, the adventures of evolution left day-to-day records, so we can travel its routes in our minds. Key episodes were preserved not only as echoes of the past in creatures turned to rock, but also in living fossils, including structures of our bodies and our minds. This is a good reason for recalling steps of evolution, for discovering where and what we are.[1]

We think and we see with analogies. Things that are unique are practically impossible to see or describe. Eyes were first understood by comparison with optical images of instruments projected on screens in the dark room especially of the magical *camera obscura*.[2] Conversely, optical instruments have been inspired by biological eyes. Writing before the photographic camera, Charles Darwin compared eyes to astronomical telescopes, and how they were designed.

Ironically, what astronomers have discovered with their eyes of glass they find almost impossible to grasp intuitively. The vast distances in space and time are too great to be encompassed in imagination, which is based on earthly experience. What is a million miles? A billion years? The astronomer can calculate the figures yet not perceive or imagine what they mean. Science stretches and often breaks free from imagination.

Changes in what can and cannot be seen as knowledge and optics advanced, applied to brains and eyes throughout their five hundred million years of evolution. We cannot appreciate the powers and limitations of eyes without considering the brains they serve; for eyes provide sensory signals but knowledge is needed to convert sensing into perceiving. So, to understand perception, we need to look at more than the optics and the physiology of sensing; we need to include knowledge that gives sensory signals meaning. We shall find that inadequate knowledge or false assumptions can have disastrous effects on seeing, as well as for understanding.

Origins of eyes and brains

Evolution is the key to the 'hardware' physiology and also the 'software' knowledge by which eyes and brains perceive objects and events. Evolution by natural selection is now the accepted key to understanding biology, yet it is still hard to conceive the immense time-span, or appreciate that we are not the product of a designing mind. For organic nature appears clearly *designed*. It is rich with answers to problems so difficult we hardly understand them. It is inconceivable that this happened simply by chance, and it didn't. Selecting from chance events is the basis of the creative 'intelligence' of evolution. It is the processes of evolution that are 'intelligent' and creative, even though they are blind and seemingly without purpose.

The evolution of eyes was seen as a special challenge to the theory of evolution, as eyes show many signs of careful, considered design. It was the complex, precise structures of eyes that gave Darwin his famous 'cold shudder'. Could eyes really arise by blind processes of trial and error, with no designer? We know from many sources that this was on Darwin's mind, as he waited anxiously for his masterpiece *The Origin of Species* to appear, late in 1859. Would his critics accept his heretical conclusions from his years of observation and thought?

To Charles Darwin—and Alfred Russel Wallace,[3] in whose joint names evolution by natural selection was announced in 1858—goes the credit for seeing that *statistical* processes invent the structures and the processes of life. This was before the mathematical field of statistics was at all fully understood, and Darwin was not a mathematician. He recognized the driving force as competition: *competition* for survival against competing individuals of various species for limited resources. There is also adaptation to natural hazards, such as drought and excessive heat. Darwin and Wallace independently realized the importance of competition from reading a book on economics by Thomas Robert Malthus (1766–1834). Malthus was a mathematician and a cleric. His *Essay on the Principle of Population* first appeared anonymously, then with extended arguments in 1803. It is truly remarkable that this book by a retiring cleric had such dramatic effects by challenging accepted explanations of religion and suggesting an immensely powerful paradigm for biology.

The claim that life forms evolve and were not pre-designed, was contentious at the time and it still is. Many people resist accepting that there was no initial plan for life, no aim or purpose in the universe.[4] Indeed intelligent design (though for obscure purpose) seems clearly supported by evidence everyone can see—the wonderful structures of plants and animals. It looked as though designing living things must have required intelligence—super-intelligence—yet Darwin revealed a blind yet super-intelligent statistical process that designed all of life, including brains and eyes, from competition for survival with limited resources.

Now, 150 years since Darwin's insight, evolution still remains so astonishing a thought it is hard to conceive in imagination. How did Darwin arrive at it? His thinking is recorded in his Notebooks. From his Notebook of 1837 it is clear that he was by then a convinced evolutionist; but in 1831, when he started his voyage on HMS Beagle, he was not convinced.[5] By 1844, fifteen years before *The Origin*, Darwin had his theory well worked out, and had considered what might challenge or refute it. He kept his 'black book' for writing down any counter-evidence that he might find. Indeed, there were difficulties and daunting gaps of evidence, and Darwin was fortunately aware of these. Why do scorpions sting themselves to death in the presence of fire? This bothered him, for how could suicide improve chances of survival? The extravagant peacock's tail was a worry: how could such an encumbrance be more useful than more a handicap? This led Darwin to another great insight: the theory of sexual selection. It is now recognized that sexual symbols can be so powerful that even such extreme examples are worth the cost. The precise, intricate structures of eyes was a challenge he took on board, though eyes did give him 'a cold shudder'.

Darwin's cold shudder

Darwin considered the evolution of eyes in his 1844 *Essay*, where he sees eyes as a special challenge.[6] Was the trial and error of natural selection adequate?[7] The theory required that there should be advantages, increasing chances of survival, at each step of the way. What could these be for the first eyes? What use is a half-formed lens? He wrote in 1844:

> In the case of the eye, as with the more complicated instincts, no doubt one's first impulse is to utterly reject every such theory. But if the eye from its most complicated form can be shown to graduate into an exceedingly simple state,—if selection can produce the smallest change, and if such a series exists, then it is clear (for in this work we have nothing to do with the first origin of organs in their simplest forms) that it might possibly have acquired by gradual selection of slight, but in each case,

useful deviations.... In the case of the eye, we have a multitude of different forms, more or less simple, not graduating into each other, but separated by sudden gaps or intervals; but we must recollect how incomparably greater would the multitude of visual structures be if we had the eyes of every fossil which ever existed.... Notwithstanding the large series of existing forms, it is most difficult even to conjecture by what intermediate stages very many simple organs could possibly have graduated into complex ones: but it should be borne in mind, that a part having originally a wholly different function, may on the theory of gradual selection be slowly worked into quite another use; the gradations of forms, from which naturalists believe in the hypothetical metamorphosis of part of the ear into the swimming bladder of fishes, and in the insects of legs into jaws, show the manner in which this is possible.

This point, that a structure may evolve for one function but come to change its use, allows a range of non-obvious benefits at intermediate stages. For example, eyes' lenses could have started out as windows protecting eye pits from filling with rubbish; gradually thickening at the centre as this usefully increases shadow contrast, to become a focusing lens. The eye's 'film' was made up of photoreceptors (rather like a digital camera), developed from ancient nerve endings sensitive to touch, touch being the primary sense, and taken over and developed for vision.

One dramatic example of modification of function is the development of the ear, from the midline organ of fish which monitors pressure and detects vibrations, to the astonishing Organ of Corti in the inner ear of vertebrates for detecting

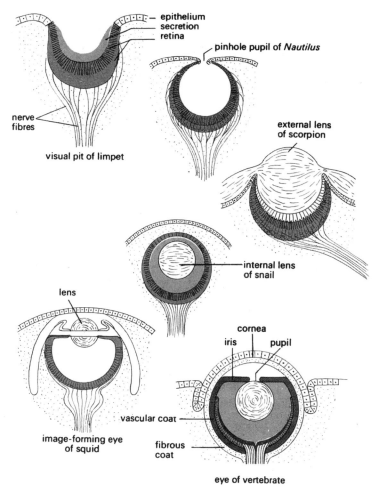

Figure 5. Evolution of eyes. From Gregory, *Eye and Brain*.

and analysing sounds. The cochlea comes from the jawbone of early fish. So, we listen to Beethoven with mechanisms designed for life in the depths of the seas. Our ears were submarine pressure organs; our tears have the salinity of ancient seas.

Touch to vision

For the start of vision, Darwin thought that any nerve could become sensitive to light–that concentrations of touch receptors became gradually more sensitive to light, and these regions became pits, increasing shadow contrast. The eye-pits became deeper, increasing shadow contrast until they closed except for a small hole, as today in *Nautilus*.[8] At this point the eye became an image-forming camera. This had dramatic consequences demanding radical re-design of the nervous system, and by warning of events distant in space and time, promoting intelligent behaviour with intelligent perception.

The shadow-image was reversed from all the touch inputs. What was up became down, right became left, and all movements were reversed from the eye's images. This had profound effects on the 'wiring' of the nervous system, effects we see now in the anatomy of the human brain, with the right brain serving the left side of the body, and the touch maps of the cortex upside down. This shortens and simplifies the cross-connections between vision and touch. The development of vision from touch maintained them as close neighbours on evolutionary journeys, with consequences to this day.

By giving early warning, eyes allow time for planning. While behaviour from touch and the other proximal senses has to be as rapid as possible, even the crudest eye gives some warning of the *future* as it probes distance. Freedom from the immediate here and now is the key to sophisticated perception, as well as to conceptual understanding. This allowed thinking to separate from perception—so imagination could take off from the here and the now, to invent new possibilities and even impossibilities.

The great size of the human brain, especially the outer cortical areas, remains an intriguing puzzle. Human brain/body weight ratio started to get greater than in other mammals about four million years ago. It is likely that this was associated with an upright stance and free use of the hands. It now seems that use of the hands drove development of the human brain. The developed brain allowed skills of the hands, leading to our unique control of the environment by tools and technology, which in turn has fed our brains with discoveries beyond the senses.

Active and passive touch—leading to 'simple' and 'compound' eyes?

There are two essentially different kinds of touch: 'passive' pattern detection, from many parallel receptors, and active 'haptic' exploratory touch with only one or a few moving receptors. There are also two essentially different kinds of eyes: 'simple' eyes, with one lens and many receptors, and 'compound' eyes with many lenses and but one neural channel for each little lens. Is there a connection here, between the two kinds of touch and the two kinds of eyes? It is tempting to extend the notion that eyes developed from the sense of touch, to suggest that the two kinds of eyes developed from the two kinds of touch.

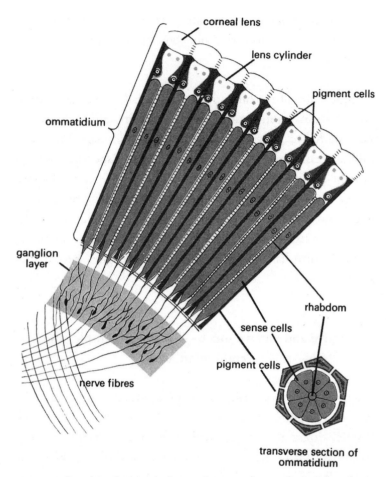

Figure 6. Simple and compound eyes. Compound eyes of insects have lower resolution for space but higher resolution for time, than simple eyes such as ours.

Each human eye has over 100,000,000 receptors in the retina, and 1,000,000 fibres in the optic nerve to the brain. The reduction takes place with 'computing' neurons in the retina, allowing the optic nerve to be thin and flexible enough for eye movements to be possible. The human retina is a vast mosaic of parallel receptors, directed by movements of the eyes to positions of interest. There is a high density of receptors in the central *fovea* of the retina, giving localized high resolution. This parallel processing is fast and efficient, but even with the concentration of the central fovea, it is costly in its complexity.

Compound eyes are very different, with their several lenses, each with a single optic nerve. Each lens points in a somewhat different direction, the insect's 'visual world' being constructed neurally.

Did simple eyes take over parallel channels, already developed for passive touch? Did compound eyes take over single-channel mechanisms, of active haptic touch? Large complicated compound eyes, such as in bees and dragonflies, have enough lenses to give parallel processing; but what of much smaller compound eyes?

Scanning eyes

Understanding structures and functions often depends on concepts developed through technology. Thus, appreciating the optical imaging of eyes required an understanding of image formation by man-made lenses. This understanding came remarkably late in the history of science, being unknown to the Greeks, and not fully appreciated before the astronomer Johannes Kepler (1571–1630), who described the details and significance of images formed in eyes such as ours, with its single lens and millions of receptors.

There is another way of producing and signalling from images. Images can be built up in time, by scanning with a moving intensity-modulated spot of light, as in television. Scanning is suitable for high-speed electronics; but we would hardly expect to find scanning in nature, with much slower neural signals. Did the many static channels of large compound eyes develop from a small number of moving, scanning receptors?[9] Is this to be found in nature?

A rare, remarkable pin-head sized Copepod, *Copilia quadrata*, was described by H. Grenacher in 1879 as having a unique eye, so strange that Grenacher did not see how it functioned. It was investigated by the distinguished German physiologist and naturalist Sigmund Exner (1846–1926) late in the nineteenth century (1891). Exner described the highly transparent and beautiful *Copilia* as having a pair of internal lens-like structures, lying deep in her pinhead-sized body, that showed *the most lively motion*. Coming across a brief account (without a picture) in *The Science of Mind and Brain* by J. S. Wilkie (1953), it made me wonder whether this could be a *scanning* eye. Though obvious to us now, with our familiarity of scanning in television, scanning might well have been opaque at that time.[10] *Copilia* seemed to have been forgotten since Exner's description of 1891. With colleagues, I determined to look for her. We set up an expedition in 1962 to try to find *Copilia* in the Bay of Naples where she had been seen seventy years before by Exner though apparently not since.[11]

Searching through several litres of teeming plankton each day with pipettes and low-power microscopes, we came near to despair of ever finding *Copilia*. Then, one day, we saw, unmistakably, a living specimen—with indeed a pair of lenses in lively motion within the remarkably transparent body. She was beautiful. The inner lenses moved in exact opposition, from a single muscle, in a saw-tooth scan-like motion.[12] The movements of this inner lens, with its single optic nerve, are 'saw-tooth' in velocity with a frequency of about 0.5 to 5 scans per second, though this is variable.[13] We found that there can be long resting periods, often with a violent burst of scanning, just before moving off. *Copilia* appears to be dead in these resting periods, as nothing moves inside. She has no heart.[14] We became convinced that this is indeed a single-channel scanning eye. But whether this was the prototype for large multi-channel compound eyes—the units multiplying, until there are enough for parallel processing—is no more than an attractive speculation. *Copilia* is not herself a direct ancestor to human beings, but she might represent a still more distant single-channel ancestral scanning eye. At least, she shows this is possible in nature.[15]

I had not read Exner's full account of *Copilia*, and assumed that he could not at that time have appreciated the concept of scanning. Recently though I have seen the English translation

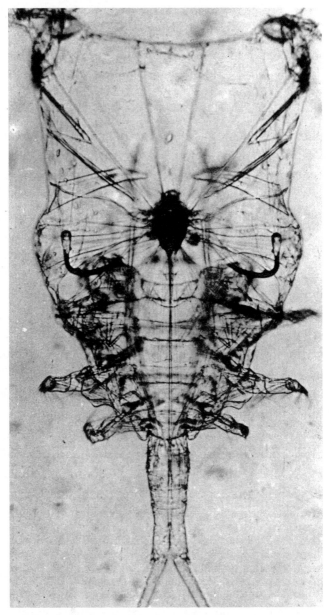

Figure 7. *Copilia quadrata*: single-channel scanning eye.

by Roger Hardie.[16] It turns out that Exner *did* appreciate scanning—by analogy with touch. He wrote:[17]

> *Copilia* thus sees by sampling the image projected by the lens with one retinal element. The psychic process underlying recognition of objects is basically the same as that we use to recognise forms by running a finger along an object and reconstructing the Gestalt form from the sequence of sensations. Such vision has a certain analogy to our perception through eye movements.

Reading the brief account in 1960 it was obvious from our familiarity with television that this could be a scanning eye. For Exner, in the nineteenth century, it was a major achievement.

What happens with eyes having just a few channels? We should expect such eyes to have oscillatory scanning movements when there are not enough channels for effective parallel processing. There are several, recently discovered, deep-sea candidates for scanning eyes having a small number of optical channels, discovered and described largely by the expert on peculiar optical systems, Michael Land.[18]

There seems to be a very familiar multi-channel scanning eye—*Daphnia*. Rather sadly, she is used for feeding goldfish, and so can be bought in pet shops, and is generally ignored. Yet *Daphnia* is much more interesting than the goldfish! With a low-power microscope, its eye of 22 ommatidia lens and receptor units, looks like a violently wiggling mulberry.[19] Isn't this *scanning*? (Figure 8).

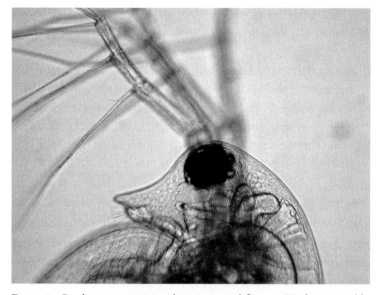

Figure 8. *Daphnia*—scanning with its 22 optical fingers? *Daphnia* is readily available in pet shops for feeding goldfish, but she is far more interesting than one might think. A low-power microscope reveals the wiggling (scanning?) 22-channel eye.

It seems that only *Copilia* has a single-channel-scanning optical finger; but she is the extreme example of several scanning eyes, invented in nature millions of years before television.[20]

The human eye

It is remarkable that the multi-channel human eye works so well though it is in continual motion; with tremor and rapid flicks 'saccades', moving rapidly from one 'fixation' to another.

Evidently perceptions are built up from fixations, the eye rotations being the fastest movements of the body.

There is also continuous oscillation, at a rate of about 30–70 Hz. It is possible that vision samples and selects the best moments for seeing. Sampling is very effective for astronomical telescopes suffering atmospheric turbulence—known as 'lucky imaging'. This was suggested and tried many years ago (Gregory 1964) but is only really effective now with high-speed electronics. We do not know how important lucky imaging is for eyes.

The human eye is general purpose, and knowledgeable, relying on its creative brain to make much from limited information. The human eye works well for 'general' vision; where the receptor rods and cones are closely spaced but which falls off from the centre—though this is hardly noticed. We are deluded into thinking we are seeing all around us clearly—for high resolution is limited to the small region of central vision, the *fovea*. The visual field is constructed from brief snapshots at each pause of the eye's continual movements. All the senses are limited, providing only restricted information about what is out there, organisms with simple brains tending to have more specialized senses tuned to their special needs. Many eyes provide only a few kinds of signals, such as of movement, with little or no information regarding form or colour. These specialized systems can in their own ways be better than ours. We cannot compete with dragonflies for seeing fast movement; but perception of form with compound eyes is crude by comparison to ours. Even the largest compound eyes have much lower acuity; though they are sensitive to shorter wave-length, ultraviolet light, which produces fairly sharp images from their small lenses.

Some species have entirely different senses, such as bats with their incredible sonar, emitting strong sound signals reflected off prey such as moths, and even from spiders' webs, which they 'see' by sound in darkness. Indeed the variety, the engineering sophistication and micro-miniaturization of sensory systems are so wonderful they are hard to believe.[21] Bat sonar makes our state-of-the-art military devices look crude by comparison.

It is interesting to simulate the senses of other creatures and try to imagine their worlds.[22] One can make simple versions of compound eyes with drinking straws, or a colander, and restrict colour vision with coloured glasses. But it is strictly impossible to experience the perceptual world of a bee or a bat. Yet there are some clues for crossing species in imagination, as from shared illusions.

The colouring of animals is unrelated to their own colour vision, but it matches the vision of animals that interact with them, especially the colour vision of their predators and mates. Flowers, of course, are coloured to appeal to insects, not to us, though we do seem to have insect-like preferences for the colours and patterns as flowers appeal so strongly to us. New Zealand's flowers are white, as there are no indigenous insects. Poisonous insects, with their typical warning red patches, have predators sensitive to red. Photographs with ultraviolet film and a UV filter give some idea of insect vision—displaced half an octave up the spectrum—showing pollen tracks on what to us are plain white flowers. Some of these invisible-to-us patterns absorb, while others reflect, ultraviolet light, to which we are blind, though insects can see them.[23]

Moths with eye-patterns on their wings have predators with form perception able to see them. These eye-pictures fool birds, though not us, suggesting that our pattern perception is more sophisticated—which is hardly surprising as our brains are so much larger. Yet we too are fooled by camouflage, such as the shape and colouring of stick insects. Certainly there are great differences of perception between species, but the commonality of many illusions links us to experience of the world hundreds of millions of years before we came on the scene without eyes and brains. Very different are our concepts and understanding, for we see in the light of human knowledge, unique in nature.

The nearest we can come to *experiencing* the evolution of vision is to look at something in central vision with our recent highly developed foveas, then look further and further away, so the image falls on ancient cells of the peripheral retina. In this time-travel of perhaps a billion years, one loses colour and then form, arriving at only movement, and simple flickering brightness. But of course this is fanciful. We can't be sure of our parent's or children's sensations, let alone the experience of ancient and much simpler creatures. Only the legal owner of eye and brain has access to phenomenal phenomena.

Notes

1. Fortunately there are many recent excellent books on the origins of species, including accounts of Darwin's life and thoughts; see, e.g. Howard E. Gruber, *Darwin on Man: Early and Unpublished Notebooks* annotated by Paul H. Barrett (New York: Dutton, 1974); and evolution and the philosophy of biology: see Richard Dawkins, *The Selfish Gene* (Oxford: Oxford University Press, 1976), *The Blind Watchmaker* (New York: Norton, 1986). For a challenging philosophical analysis, see Daniel C. Dennett, *Dangerous Idea* (London: Allen Lane, Penguin Press, 1995).

2. Optical images were unknown to the Greeks. The first account of a *camera obscura* was the experiments with pinholes by Ibn Al-Haytham (Alhazen) in the tenth century. Giavanni Battista Della Porta (1543–1615), though not the first, made well known the use of lenses in a *camera obscura* in his *Natural Magic* (1589), which relates it to the eye. Scheiner (1630) revealed retinal images in cow's eyes by removing the outer coating, described also by Descartes in 1664.

3. At the Linnean Society in London, on 1 July 1858, Alfred Russel Wallace (1823–1913) had a remarkably similar experience; Malthus also inspired him. He collected specimens in the Malay Archipelago, and the Amazon Basin. (1848–52). Much of his collection was lost in a disastrous fire on board ship. He wrote to Darwin with the idea of the survival of the fittest, twenty years after Darwin started work on it—prodding Darwin into completing *The Origin of Species*.

4. *The Origin of Species* was burned in many southern states of America, and until very recently lessons on evolution were banned from schools in Alabama.

5. According to his son Francis Darwin, writing in 1906: 'On his departure in 1831, Henslow gave him vol. 1 of Lyell's *Principles* [*of Geology*], then just published, with the warning that he was not to believe what he read. But believe it he did, and it is certain (as Huxley has forcibly pointed out) that the doctrine of uniformitarionism when applied to Biology leads of necessity to Evolution. If the extermination of a species is no more

catastrophic than the natural death of an individual, why should the birth of a species be any more miraculous than the birth of an individual? It is quite clear that this thought was vividly present to Darwin when he was writing out his early thoughts in the 1837 Note Book: "If *species* generate other *species*, their race is not utterly cut off." '

6. In the section 'Difficulties in the acquirement by Selection of complex corporeal structure'.

7. The term 'survival of the fittest' was coined by Herbert Spencer in 1852.

8. The development and involvement of the brain for vision is well described by H. B. Sarnat and M. G. Netsky in *Evolution of the Nervous System* (New York: Oxford University Press, 1974/81), 29:

Eyes and olfactory receptors developed early in the evolution of vertebrates. These structures are already differentiated in the most primitive of living vertebrates, the cyclostomes. Tactile perception and taste give information about the distant or remote environment. The importance of distant information is evidenced by the evolution of the phylogenetic series of vertebrates, contrasted with the failure of creatures lacking distance receptors to evolve further, exemplified by amphioxus.

The anatomical organization of the nervous system established in the hypothetical ancestral vertebrate was repeated and expanded in all subsequent vertebrates. That basic pattern involving specialization of the hindbrain for receiving information about the immediate environment, and of the midbrain and forebrain for receiving information about the distant environment. Sensory impulses related to touch, temperature, taste, and balance thus entered the medulla for quick reflexive responses by motor nuclei. Information from distance receptors, however, entered the midbrain from the eyes, or the forebrain from the olfactory epithelium. Because the distance from the object perceived by sight or smell was greater, more time was available before motor responses were required, so that a longer delay in conducting impulses to medullar motor centres was not a disadvantage. Remote information also required more interpretation before responses were made, and the forebrain therefore became more associative while the medulla remained reflexive. With the further evolution of the forebrain, all sensory information eventually was relayed rostrally for interpretation and correlation, but the primitive medullar reflexes persist, even in man.

Although it is true that subtle brain-processing of optical images enormously increases the usefulness of eyes, it is not quite true to say they have *no* use without neural 'interpreting' to give meaningful perception of objects. Sensing distant movement, for example, is useful, even though the source of the movement is not recognized, for movement is often associated with danger and so it signals probable danger. (It is noteworthy that many radar systems reject stationary echoes, allowing only moving 'targets' to be visible.)

9. Although this works fine with the high speeds of electronic components, biological receptors and neural channels are far too slow for efficient scanning; so it is not surprising if scanning eyes became multi-channel parallel systems.

10. The principle of converting one-dimension into two dimensions, with a time-series of signals, was invented by F. C. Bakewell in about 1850, for his Copying Telegraph (Bakewell 1853); but it was not well known, or its significance at all generally appreciated, until considerably after 1884 when Paul Nipkow invented the scanning disk, which became the heart of Baird's mechanical television of the 1930s. We may assume that the principle of sending spatial information down a single channel by scanning would not have been known to Exner at that time; so it would not be surprising that he failed at first to recognize it as an eye, and never understood it.

Here is the translation of part of Exner's 1891 paper, (Wilkie 1953):

Copilia, which I have had the opportunity of examining living and dead ... is a Copepod of a few millimetres in length flattened from above downwards, and seen from above about the shape of an isosceles triangle. The narrow base of this triangle is formed by the front edges of the animal, and at either end of this edge is a strikingly beautiful lens ... Grenacher has observed, and I can confirm, that the lens is composed of two substances: one cuticular, which itself has the form of a concavo-convex lens; and one posterior to this which is a powerful biconvex lens. The lenses are the most anterior parts of the whole animal, and behind them is not, as one would have expected, a retina, but transparent parts of the body. Only far behind, about half the length of the body away, does one discover a structure which at first one does not at all recognize as related to the lens. It is a crystalline body having the form of a cone, rounded in front, with high refractive power, superposed upon a yellow rod. . . . This rod is the only pigmented part of the animal's body. The crystalline cone is anchored anteriorly by suspensory liga-ments, which extend to the region the lens. Laterally, a nerve enters the yellow rod, and this is the optic nerve. Also a striated muscle is attached to the rod.

The yellow rod showed the most lively movements, which were remarkably constant. The rods of the two eyes were drawn towards the median plane or moved from it together, and, as far as could be seen without measurements, they remained at the same distance from the lenses. I found by micrometer that in the living animal the distance between the posterior pole of the lens and the convexity of the crystalline cone was 0.87 mm. . . . I cut a narrow slice from the anterior extremity of the animal, and was able to arrange this in the water at such an angle that the hinder surface of the lens was turned towards the objective of the microscope. In this way one sees a surprisingly beautiful image thrown by the lens. Its distance from the posterior pole of the lens I found to be 0.93 mm.

11. Professor J. Z. (John) Young, then Head of the Department of Anatomy at University College London, kindly arranged for labora-tory space at the Zoologica Stazioni, with collection of specimens by laboratory staff. I was joined by Neville Moray (an Oxford zoologist and psychologist) and Helen Ross (a graduate student working with me on perceptual problems of astronauts). Our knowledge and experience of this kind of work was extremely limited.

12. The first strange thing about *Copilia quadrata* is that, though a Copepod, she is not of 'oar-foot' shape. She is squared in front, with her two huge anterior lenses like car headlamps—hence very appropriately *quadrata*. *Copilia* is also appropriate, for she is evocatively beautiful, and all her charms are visible as she is perhaps

uniquely transparent. Indeed, she is exceedingly hard to see, and is easily lost even within the confines of a Petrie dish. The female *Copilia* is 5–6 mm in length, and about 1 mm in width. She has two huge anterior lenses, which are fixed, the moving inner lens of each eye being attached to a 'rod' photoreceptor, which is curved inwards, like a hockey stick. The receptor is orange in colour, this being the only pigment of this extraordinarily transparent creature, in which all the inner structure is clearly visible with a low-power microscope.

13. A saw-tooth motion should be expected for scanning, the scanned information coming from the slow movement as the fast is discarded, to avoid erroneous overlap.

14. Some Copepods have a heart, others not. They are classified from distinguishing features of dead specimens; but the non-beating heart is hard to see, so is not included in definitions of 'Copepod'.

15. I am indebted to Michael Land for this information. The recent book (2002) *Animal Eyes* by M. F. Land and D.-E. Nilsson (Oxford: Oxford University Press) is delightful.

16. Roger C. Hardie and Sigmund Exner, *The Physiology of the Compound Eyes of Insects and Crustaceans* (Berlin: Springer-Verlag, 1989), 93–7. Translated from the (unattainable) German original: *Die Physiologie der facettierten Augen von Krebsen und Insecten* (1891).

17. Hardie (1989: 96).

18. M. F. Land (1988) 'The functions of the eye and body movements in *Labidocer* and other copepods', *J.Exp. Biol.* 140: 381–91. Further references to Land's work are in R. L. Gregory, 'Origins of eyes— with speculations on scanning eyes'., in *Evolution of the Eye and Visual System.* Vol. 2 *Vision and Visual Dysfunction*, ed. John R. Cronley-Dillon and Richard L. Gregory (London: Macmillan, 1991), 52–9. This contains many technical articles on evolution of eyes.

19. Human eye movements are not, in this technical sense, scanning. Human eyes move in rapid jerks (saccades), which serve just the opposite of scanning. They are so rapid they prevent information uptake during the movement. When the human eye follows a target

in motion, however, the eye movements are not saccadic jerks; but are smooth, allowing continuous uptake of information. Neither kind of eye movement is scanning—it is directing the mosaic of receptors to different regions for simultaneous parallel processing by the brain.

20. A large marine Copepod, *Labidocera* was described by Parker (1891). The male's eye was described as having two retinas, that may be rotated on their lenses through an angle of about forty-five degrees: '. . . by contraction of the posterior muscle, the retina may be drawn upward and backward over the surface of the lens, till its axis, instead of pointing dorsally, is directed forward and upward at an angle of about forty-five degrees with its original position. The retina is not usually held for any length of time in this position, but is soon returned by the contraction of the anterior muscle to its normal place. The backward motion of the retina is accomplished with such rapidity that the animal has the appearance of winking.' These observations are essentially confirmed, and extended by Michael Land (1988). He finds that the movement occur 'in bouts, lasting from a few seconds to a minute, often with many minutes between bouts.'

21. For the diverse senses of many species, see Howard C. Hughes, *Sensory Exotica*. (Cambridge MA: MIT Press, 1999). The standard reference for vertebrate eyes is Gordon L. Walls, *The Vertebrate Eye and its Adaptive Radiation*. (New York: Hafner, 1942).

22. The impossibility of imagining the sensory worlds of other animals is superbly described by the American philosopher Thomas Nagel (1974), 'What is it like to be a bat?' *The Philosophical Review*, October. See Douglas R. Hoffstadter, and Daniel C. Dennett, *The Mind's Eye* (New York: Basic Books, 1945).

23. Ultraviolet vision of insects is described and illustrated by Howard Hinton (1973), 'Natural Deception', in *Illusion in Nature and Art*, ed. R. L Gregory and E. H. Gombrich (London: Duckworth), 97–159.

CHAPTER 4

UNLOCKING LOCKE

We are interested here in *phenomenal* phenomena rather than phenomena of the physical world. We think of the brain as a physical system handling mental symbols. This goes back to the seventeenth-century English philosopher John Locke (1632–1704). A friend of Newton, Locke set out to bridge the philosophy and science of his day with views and arguments that remain of great interest.

Locke held many of the keys to our views, especially the concept that objects around us are not as they appear. Locke and Newton appreciated that although objects appear coloured there is no colour in objects, or indeed in light. They realized that colours are created in brains; so there would be no colours in the universe, without suitable eyes and brains to create them.

Writing in his *Opticks* of 1704 (the year of Locke's death), Newton said that red light is not itself red, but is *red-making*, green is *green-making*, and so on for all colours we see. Newton expressed this in the strongest terms:

And if at any time I speak of Light and Rays as coloured or embued with Colours, I would be understood to speak not philosophically and properly, but grossly, and according to such Conceptions as vulgar People in seeing all these Experiments would be apt to frame. For the Rays to speak properly are not coloured. In them there is nothing else but a certain Power and Disposition to stir up a Sensation of this or that Colour.

Yet surfaces of objects do *appear* to be coloured. It is a startling idea that psychologically we *project* colours, created in our brains, into the world of colourless objects. How much of what we see is *received* from the object world, and how much is *created* by the brain? Phenomena of illusions are tools for finding out what is in the external reality of objects and what is created in the brain's virtual reality of mind.

John Locke discusses this in his *Essay Concerning Human Understanding* (1690). He tried to distinguish between what he called primary *(objective)* and secondary *(subjective)* qualities of things. But separating these turned out to be surprisingly difficult, some philosophers would say impossible. In *A History of Western Philosophy* (1946), Bertrand Russell says of Locke that although he is not always right, he is 'the most fortunate of all philosophers',[1] for:

Not only Locke's valid opinions, but even his errors were useful in practice. Take, for example, his doctrine as to primary and secondary qualities. The primary qualities are defined as those that are inseparable from body, and are enumerated as solidity, extension, figure (shape), motion or rest, and number. The secondary qualities are all the rest: colours, sounds, smells, etc. The primary qualities, he maintains, are actually in bodies [objects]; the secondary qualities, on the contrary, are only in the percipient. Without the eye, there would no colours; without the ear, no sounds, and so on.

Russell agrees that there are grounds for secondary qualities, though as Bishop George Berkeley (1685–1753) pointed out, much the same arguments apply to primary qualities. Russell says, 'Ever since Berkeley, Locke's dualism on this point has been philosophically out of date.' Russell goes on to say of Locke's attempted distinction between primary and secondary qualities for separating mind and matter:[2]

> The theory that the physical world consists only of matter in motion was the basis of the accepted theories of sound, heat, light, and electricity. Pragmatically, the theory was useful, however mistaken it may have been theoretically. This is typical of Locke's doctrines.

Bertrand Russell's own account of perception is what is called Neutral Monism: the idea that perceptions are made of a substance, neither matter nor mind, but lying between them. He was writing before the impact computers now have on mind-matter debates. It would be interesting to know what Russell would think now of mind as software run by the hardware (squishyware) of the physical brain. Would he favour this over Neutral Monism? He might say that computer software provides only a pale account of mind, having no place for sensations or secondary qualities.

As is very well known, the Irish philosopher George Berkeley (1685–1753) denied the existence of matter.[3] Or rather, he denied matter's existence when not being perceived. He did admit, though, that a fire would warm an empty room—so the fire must exist though no person is seeing it. He said that God must be seeing the fire in the empty room, allowing matter hidden from us to exist. But didn't he cheat with God?—by saying (in the words of Ronald Knox) that, 'When there's no one about in the quad, the tree will continue to be, since observed by yours faithfully, God.'

As Berkeley became a Bishop, this might have seemed a strong defence, though for the rest of us surely it is not. One might ask: Who observes God—to make Him exist? If the observer is not necessary for God's existence, why should observing be necessary for matter to exist? However this may be, Berkeley did put forward powerful arguments that have been debated ever since, against Locke's separation of primary and secondary qualities. A problem is that what seems to be primary or secondary depends on the theory of perception that is held, and may change as the physical sciences strive to reach an understanding of the nature of matter.

Locke's main evidence for separating appearance from reality was from phenomena of illusions. As Berkeley pointed out, objects appear smaller at a distance, and they change shape as we walk around them—yet size and shape were supposed to be primary qualities in objects—not secondary qualities in the observer. So how can primary and secondary be essentially different?

The sense of touch seems the most direct and most reliable of the senses. But (as Berkeley also pointed out) if one puts one hand in hot water and the other in cold, and then both in tepid water; this will at the same time feel hot and cold. But it is impossible for an object to be hot and cold at the same time. Hence this *perception* would be impossible if perceptions were directly related to objects. If Locke's primary-secondary dualism is correct, even though just what is primary or secondary may be questioned, these difficulties disappear.

Dualisms, however, generally get a bad press from modern philosophers, such as Dan Dennett.[4] Descartes' mind-brain dualism is seen as especially misleading. So, can we accept Locke's dualism of physical reality and psychological appearance? I think we can, and the evidence supports it. The separation of vision from the world of objects was dramatized with the discovery of pictures in eyes—retinal images—that give us sight though they are never seen.

Meaning

Meaning is hard to define, and so far impossible to measure. One might say that the present is perceived with meaning from analogies with past experience. So events, objects, pictures and language have greater meaning as knowledge grows with experience. This includes emotional meanings. Pictures are 'read' from knowledge of objects gained from interacting with them in various situations. So, amazingly, a splodge of paint is seen as something very different—say, a weeping woman.

The meaning is projected on to the splodge from past experi-ence of women and weeping. Conversely, art may increase the meaning of life's experiences, by concentrating the atten-tion and providing new contexts and suggesting new questions. Thus: Why is the paint-splodge woman in the picture weeping? Would other women, or men, weep in this supposed situation? Is she weeping to court our sympathy? Am I, the viewer, responding as I should? Generally, increased experience and education raise ability to read meanings into art, and allow art to increase the meaning of experience. But pictures would be meaningless—mere splodges—without knowledge of objects and how they affect us in various situations.

Different meanings are read for different uses. Knowledge is typically geared for uses, but these may be very different from one individual to another, or for the same individual at different times. Such differences may be dramatic between artists and scientists, as their knowledge bases are so different, and used differently. Communication between art and science is not easy, though it is rewarding. Surely for artists significance is *individual* meaning; though for science, more significant is shared knowledge, accepted as objective.

So far, we need human beings to read meanings. However, computers are catching up. My guess is that when machines can handle information organized as knowledge they, like us, will function through meaning. Then AI will really take off, with unpredictable consequences. Their meanings are likely to be very different from ours.

Significance

It can be as important to see the *significance* of a phenomenon as to discover it. An example is Newton seeing the significance of glass prisms producing rainbow colours. It was already known that a prism would produce colours (that he named red, orange, yellow, green, blue, indigo, violet) from white sunlight. Newton was able to buy his long narrow glass prisms at a fair in Cambridge, as they were sold to produce sparkling colours for chandeliers. Newton's genius was to ask why this happened and realize that the colours were not in the glass but in the light—separated and laid out in sequence by refraction of the prism. Newton saw the significance of already known phenomena for understanding light and colour in a new way.

Why are some phenomena especially significant? To be interesting for science, observations and experiments should have two kinds of significance: *conceptual* significance and *statistical* significance. They should be surprising yet accepted as genuine. The same holds for explanations: they should be surprising yet believable. We will be most concerned here with *conceptual* significance—with what phenomena may *mean*. The reliability of information is, however, vital for science, and must not be assumed. Here, though, almost all the phenomena occur without serious doubt. What is interestingly in doubt is how they should be explained, and what they suggest. This depends on background knowledge and assumptions that may be controversial. The reader might well disagree with some of the interpretations I suggest here, perhaps coming up with better accounts, which would be progress.

The more unlikely an observation, or result of an experiment, the more information it conveys. But if too unlikely it will not be believed. There is a quite narrow range of probabilities for accepting an observation or explanation as sufficiently likely to be accepted as true and sufficiently surprising to be interesting.

To say this again: when the result of an experiment is completely expected it conveys no information; when too unlikely it will not be believed. In our culture (our shared knowledge and assumptions) this is so for ghosts and miracles, which are just too unlikely to justify time and money to investigate. If they were true, however, they would be immensely important. They would convey so much information we would have to think very differently about matter and mind, and what the brain does. For some, this justifies taking them seriously. For others, the chance of finding gold is simply too low. These judgements are the art of science.

Notes

1. Bertrand Russell, *A History of Western Philosophy* (New York: Simon & Schuster, 1945), 629.
2. Russell, *History of Western Philosophy*, 630.
3. The Irish philosopher George Berkeley was born near Kilkenny and educated at Trinity College Dublin, where he wrote his *Essay on a New Theory of Vision* (1709), arguing that ideas come from habitual sensations. He lived for a few years in America and became Bishop of Cloyne in Ireland.
4. Cf. D. C. Dennett, *Consciousness Explained* (Boston, MA: MIT Press, 1991).

CHAPTER 5

KINDS AND CAUSES

A major aim of this book is to present phenomena of vision with discussions of how they may be explained and classified, by kinds and causes. The classification starts with *physical* causes of optics, moving on to *physiological* disturbances of neural signals, and then to *cognitive* processes, in which the brain makes sense of sensory signals with rules and knowledge, though sometimes getting it wrong.

Cognitive processes divide into two kinds: general *rules* and more specific *knowledge* of objects and situations. Perception is active making sense of the senses, for immediate behaviour and for planning into the future.

The hyphen in 'physiological-psychology'

The distinction between *physiological* and *cognitive* is not straightforward or free from controversy. One might say, in the most general terms, that this is the distinction between how a machine *works* and what it *does*. The brain is a machine and this applies to all machines. For example, a can-opener needs two descriptions: the mechanism of levers and cutters, and what this does to open a can. It works for some cans though not for others. An intelligent can opener would assess the can and change its own states to cope with each kind. This could need 'software' knowledge and rules for the 'hardware' to deal with the various cans and situations. The hardware-software distinction is clearest for computers and most important for brain and mind.

How are processes of physiology related to mind? In other words, what is the hyphen in 'physiological-psychology'? Phenomena such as the placebo effect (benefit from a dummy pill believed to be the real thing) suggests close connections between physiology and psychology. It greatly matters whether the traumatic symptoms of schizophrenia are best controlled by words or by drug therapy. Here the physiology-psychology distinction is not 'merely academic'—but academic discussions can lead to improved therapy.

Truths from illusions

An illusion may be due to some *physical* optical disturbance, before the eye is reached, or it may be a *physiological* failure in the eye or brain. Or subtly different—it may be *misreading* of good sensory signals.[1] Whether and how sensory signals are misread may depend on the situation, for perception depends very much on context.

A crucially important distinction, as I have noted before, is between *bottom-up* signals from the senses and *top-down* knowledge from the brain. Some illusions are 'bottom-up' signalling errors, others are 'top-down' misreading of signals or data. Though very different conceptually, these can be hard to identify in practice.

Pictures

Visual research often uses pictures, though pictures are not typical objects, and are very odd as they convey *other objects*, in a different space and time. Rather than calling pictures illusions, however, it seems better to say they *allude* to other objects.[2]

Only paintings with effective Trompe l'Oeil (or highly realistic photographs) give retinal images approximating to images from normal objects. It is nearly always obvious that we are looking at a picture, and yet we accept it as representing or *alluding* to other objects, such as people or buildings and so on, in their own space and time. So pictures have a double reality. They are things we look at, but see far more than is physically present.

It is most strange that people seen in pictures seem almost alive, and with personalities, about to move and speak. Our knowledge of people gives life to the dead canvas, and the stone or metal statue.

Sensations

Physiological studies tell us that some brain regions give vision, others hearing, and so on for touch and smell and the other senses. The signals from the senses to the brain are all physically the same—minute pulses of electricity, increasing in frequency with increasing intensity of stimulation.[3] What matters is which regions of brain are stimulated. If the nerves from the eyes were switched over with the ears, their sets of nerves going to each other's brain regions, we would hear sounds when light entered the eyes and see colours when the ears were stimulated with sounds.[4]

This principle—that each of the senses gives its own kind of sensation, according to which region of the brain is simulated—was recognized early in the nineteenth century by the founding father of modern physiology, Johannes Müller.[5] Johannes Müller (1801–58) called this the *Law of Specific Energies*. This is a clumsy name. Why 'energies'? Why a 'Law'? Possibly because its name is so clumsy, this important brain-mind concept is often ignored or forgotten. Let's call it Müller's 'Sensational Principle'.

When the usual divisions of sensory qualities break down, cross-sensory illusions of synaesthesia are experienced. For example, sounds may be coloured. More familiar for most of us, we experience colours when we press our eyes, very gently. Then *pressure* activates the *light* receptors, so a wrong part of the brain is stimulated and we *see* this *touch*. Most remarkably, if eyes are connected to the auditory brain, this region gradually changes its anatomy to be like the structure of the visual cortex. Whether it is visual signals, or perhaps some chemical signal, that transforms this region, is not known.

Relating brain regions to kinds of sensations is a beginning, but does not tell us anything of how the brain works to create sensations. We know more and more about *where* but almost nothing of *how* (or indeed *why*) we have sensations. Recent techniques of brain imaging with magnetic resonance (fMRI) are giving exciting results. Like any other techniques or experimental observations they need to be *interpreted*—a process that often calls upon experiments and ideas at first unrelated. This makes predicting or planning science almost impossibly difficult.

Kinds and causes of illusions

We learn a great deal about perception when it departs from the world of objects, when we have illusions. I illusions are phenomena—phenomena of perception—and we can classify them, much as we can classify physical phenomena. Just as it is rewarding to put physical phenomena in their place by classifying, so this should help us to understand illusions, and so perception itself. We have already suggested *kinds of illusions*, so we may now introduce a tentative structure with examples. This will be our 'Peeriodic Table' of illusions and their causes (Table 1, p. 90–91). Kinds of causes are shown in italics (For the full 'Peeriodic Table' see Table 2, p. 242).

Notes

1. To take a contemporary example to illustrate this: if a train driver passes what should be a signal at red; the signal may have failed, or he may have failed to see it. Putting this into the nervous system, the eyes and other senses send signals to the brain. If something goes wrong, this may be because the neural signal has failed to reach the brain (without distortion or other error) or the brain has failed to make sense of the signal. This may be because the brain's physiology is malfunctioning, or because sensory signals are being read from false assumptions inappropriate knowledge. Although this physiology-cognitive distinction is basic, it is not always easy to make. Physiological and cognitive errors can be surprisingly similar. For example, distortions of either kind are distortions of length, curvature, size, distance, and so on—though the causes are fundamentally different. Quite subtle experiments may be needed to decide which kind of distortion a given illusion phenomenon is. This is often controversial among experts—naturally, physiologists favouring physiological explanations and psychologists favouring cognitive explanations! There is a pride in 'owning' interesting phenomena.

2. The psychologist Nicholas Wade uses 'allusions' in this way.

3. This has been known since about 1910, especially through the work of Lord Adrian at Cambridge (Douglas Adrian, 1st Baron, (1889–1977). See A. D. Adrian's *The Basis of Sensation* (1928), and *The Mechanisms of Nervous Action* (1932) (both Cambridge: Cambridge University Press).

4. This has essentially been done with ferrets. See L. Melchner, S. L. Pallas, M. Sur (2000) 'Visual behaviour mediated by retinal projections directed to the auditory pathway', *Nature* 404/6780 (20 April): 871–6. Comment in: *Nature* (2000) 404/6780 (20 April): 820–1.

5. Actually Müller was anticipated by Sir Charles Bell (1774–1842), though Müller gets the credit, perhaps because he appreciated its importance more fully.

Table 1. PEERIODIC TABLE OF ILLUSIONS

KINDS OF ILLUSIONS	KINDS OF CAUSES			
	PHYSICAL		COGNITIVE	
	Optics	*Signals*	*Rules*	*Knowledge*
Blindness	Dim light *e.g. Cataract of the lens*	Retinal damage *e.g. loss of blood supply*	*Perceptual hypotheses rejected when inconsistent*	Agnosia *Patterns without meaning*
Confounded Ambiguity	Low contrast *Insignificant difference of photon rates*	Neural *noise Random noise masks signals*	Camouflage Gestalt *Laws of organization combine objects incorrectly*	Differences Ignored *as meaningless* PROTOAGNOSIA *Faces continued*
Flipping Ambiguity	Quantum jumps *Uncertainty*	Retinal rivalry Stereo *fusion fails*	Necker cube, Duck-Rabbit Switching *alternative hypotheses, when probabilities are equal*	Hollow head *Faces are convex—so low probability for a hollow mask*
Instability	Laser light *Interference*	Ouchi figure *Border locking fails* (?)	Dot patterns *Many hypotheses entertained with inadequate rules or knowledge*	Thatcher illusion *Violates knowledge for important rapid recognition*

Distortion	Stick-in-water *Refraction of light*	Café Wall *Border locking across 'mortar lines'*	Ponzo, Muller-Lyer *Inappropriate size scaling*	Body image *Social pressure?*
Fiction	Rainbows *Dispersion of light*	After-image *Stored photo-chemical energy*	Kanizsa triangle *Gaps accepted as evidence of nearer occluding objects*	Ghosts *Human figures very likely— accepted with little evidence*
Paradox	Mirror reversal *Rotation of object, or head, and eyes to face the mirror*	After-effects *e.g. adapting a parallel channel—so motion seen without change of position*	Penrose triangle *Touching ends assumed to be same distance though they are not*	Magritte mirror painting *Face expected in the mirror—so shock of surprise at seeing back of head*

BLINDNESS: NO SENSATION TO NO SENSE

It might seem strange to introduce phenomena of vision with *no* vision, yet where else should we begin? Long-term eye blindness means no *sensation*s of light or colour. This loss can occur with cataract cutting off the light, or damage to the retina, especially loss of blood supply. It can also occur with lesions of the brain. There is also mind-blindness—known as *agnosia*—when sensations of light and colour, movement, and also of form are present yet lacking meaning. Objects are seen as more-or-less meaningless patterns. So, we move from no sensations to no sense.

The illusion of blindness is, of course, that nothing seems to exist. One can try to capture the experience simply by closing one's eyes. Then, although objects persist for touch they cease to exist for sight; hence the drama for children of the game peek-a-boo. Now things exist—now they don't. As Francis Bacon (1561–1626) said, 'Men fear death as children fear to go into the dark; and as that natural fear in children is increased with tales, so is the other.' But long-term blindness is not the same as experiencing black, or pitch-black darkness. For sighted people black is a sensation, a colour. Blindness is *lack* of visual sensation, which is very different from seeing black. The *nothingness* of blindness can be imagined by sighted people by attending to the unseen world behind one's head. Here there is *no* sensation—very different from experiencing the black of darkness that we see by closing the eyes or switching off the light.

Black is a colour, and like other colours it is enhanced by contrast. It is interesting that a television screen is far from black when it is switched off, yet regions of jet-black are seen in its picture when switched on, though the electron beam always adds light. This is a neat demonstration of the importance of contrast, in space and time, needed for seeing black—or indeed for seeing anything.

What is it like to become blind? John Hull described this most eloquently in his remarkable book *Touching the Rock* (1991). He tells us how different it is from being blindfolded, as blind people 'see' with their hands: 'As long as the blind person has one free hand, he sees with that hand. He does not experience not knowing where to go or where he is so long as he can guide himself with his free hand.'[1] The immediate loss of a sense, as by blindfolding, is very different from long-term loss—when other senses and new strategies come into play.

Recovering from blindness

Rare cases of recovery from blindness from birth, or from infancy, are not only remarkably interesting as personal stories, they are important for throwing light on the nature of perception. I was fortunate to study such a case—the case of 'SB'—forty years ago, with my colleague Jean Wallace.[2] Earlier cases had been described, but almost all were blind with cataract, receiving sight by removal of the lenses, which gives slow recovery of sight, because the eyes need weeks or months to recover from the operation. SB was blind because his corneas were opaque, from 10 months and probably from birth. He received corneal grafts giving retinal images immediately, at the age of 52.[3]

A few minutes after the bandages were removed, following initial confusion, he could see some things and name them. We found that he could see things he had known by touch while blind. But he could not make sense of things he had been unable to touch. These he saw as meaningless patterns. This dependence on earlier touch experience for extracting meaning from his new sense seems highly suggestive.

Normally objects are seen as far more than patterns, though patterns of shapes and colours and movements are all that eyes signal to the brain. We experience more characteristics of things than can be signalled visually: heavy, hard, blunt, sharp, pleasant, disgusting, and so on. These additions to optical features come from knowledge of objects, knowledge largely derived from the other senses and from interacting with things.

For seeing things as objects, rather than merely as patterns, it is essential to *know* about solidity, hardness, squishiness, heaviness, and so on. We see a paperweight as very different from a jelly, because in past experience we have handled hard and heavy things and tasted wobbly jellies.

This knowledge from handling and tasting and hearing things is carried into pictures—which of course are not touched or tasted. Yet a painted paperweight looks quite hard, a jelly quite wobbly. This must be from having interacted with such things over many years. Most curiously, at another level or in another part of the brain, we know *intellectually* that we are looking at splodges of pigment in a picture and yet we *see* them as paperweights, jellies, people, and so on. SB made almost nothing of pictures. Pictures, especially cartoons, irritated him as he strived for meaning he could not find.

We realized that SB could see remarkably well what he already knew from touch, when he told us the time from a clock in the hospital ward. Thinking he must have known or guessed the time, we borrowed an alarm clock from a nurse and set its hands to arbitrary times. SB read the times correctly without difficulty. How could he do this if he had really been blind? We soon discovered that he had learned to tell the time by touch. He had carried a large 'hunter' pocket watch in his top jacket pocket. His watch had no glass, and the front case opened so that he could feel its hands. He demonstrated that he could quickly and easily tell the time by touching the hands of his watch. Evidently, this knowledge from previous touch experience was available for his new vision. This struck me then as remarkably interesting, and still does.

There were many other examples of 'transfer' from touch to vision. SB could immediately read upper-case (capital) letters by sight, though not lower-case letters, having been taught upper-case though (fortunately for us) not lower-case letters by touch when he was a boy in the blind school.[4] He saw familiar things—tables and chairs, then buses and animals, and so on—from his earlier touch experience. But he was effectively blind for things he knew nothing about.

Upon leaving the hospital we took him to London, starting with the zoo. Figure 9 shows his drawing of an elephant from his imagination a few minutes before we showed him this magnificent creature.

How did he know about elephants? When he was a boy, the family had a large dog, and his mother (he and his elder sister told me) described an elephant as like the dog—but with a tail at both ends. Strangely, when we showed him the elephant he at first ignored it. He seldom found things strange or interesting, though took delight in brightness and colour, and also movement, as in the pigeons in Trafalgar Square. SB was terrified of traffic. We had to drag him across the road, though when blind he would raise his white cane and charge across without fear. Most strikingly, in the Science Museum we showed SB a simple lathe—a tool he knew about and which he wished he could use. At first he was confused, then, running his hand over it he said, 'Now I have touched it I can see'.

Figure 9. SB's drawing of an elephant, drawn from imagination a few days after receiving sight. Drawing made in the London zoo.

We may conclude that the sense of touch is the primary source of information of forms and uses of objects. Without knowledge, initially from handling and interacting with objects, it is practically impossible for the brain to make sense of vision—to see.

There are some twenty fully reported examples of adult recovery from early blindness, the most recent being MM, in California, who was blinded in an accident at the age of three. He was given corneal grafts, with the aid of stem cells when forty-three years of age. His experiences and the findings of the scientists studying him are very similar to SB; though in addition MM received functional brain imaging—showing brain impairment of form processing and object and face recognition.[5] The functional imaging showed normal brain processing for motion. MM could use motion to reveal three-dimensional shapes, such as a Necker Cube, that (like SB) he could not see as two-dimensional, or as 'flipping'. Again like SB, MM found no distortion in perspective illusions. Also often he could only recognize an object visually after touching it.

MM is making excellent use of his limited vision (less than SB's), though like SB he can find it disturbing. From being a champion blind skier, now he will only ski downhill with his eyes shut!

What do babies know?

Very young babies have some innate, but almost no learned knowledge. As their behaviour is so limited, it is hard to discover just what they know innately but there is a wealth of interesting current research on the dawn of perception, with ingenious experiments. It is found that touch exploration starts even before birth.[6]

A key technique for finding out what babies know is to note what *surprises* them. If they are surprised at an object falling obliquely, this would be evidence that they have some prior knowledge that things fall vertically. If an object disappears behind a screen to re-appear as a different object (such as a teddy bear turning into a fire engine), surprise would suggest that they have innate knowledge that objects do not generally turn into other objects. (This is known as 'object permanence'.) Another technique is to watch where they look. Very young babies spend more time looking at a simple drawing of a face, than at a drawing having the same features but moved around into a jumbled face. This shows that babies have some innate knowledge of faces, no doubt as they are such important objects for survival; but of course, they have to learn to distinguish their mother's from other faces. They do this very soon. Some learning in infants is so rapid it can be hard to know what is learned and what is already known innately.

Adapting

Sensation is gradually lost with continuous stimulation. This is a simple kind of adaptation, which is not under voluntary control, and occurs in the periphery of the nervous system before the brain is reached. Adaptation can also be cortical and can be related to attention, so partly under voluntary control. Gradual loss of sensory signals by peripheral adaptation was beautifully described by the pioneering physiologist E. D. (later Lord) Adrian, in *The Basis of Sensation* (1928). On going to sleep, Adrian writes:[7]

> If the organism were motionless the phasic receptors would discharge impulses whenever the environment changed, but would cease to do so as soon as it had settled down to a steady condition. We take advantage of this when we are going to sleep, for the usual method consists in turning out the light, shutting out sounds as far as possible, arranging ourselves in bed so that all the muscles are relaxed, and then keeping quite still.
>
> Our consciousness of our body and its environment fades rapidly and sooner or later we go to sleep. This is a good example of the fact that the skin receptors become very rapidly adapted to a

constant environment. The pressure receptors and the muscle receptors continue to discharge under constant stimulation but we stop the latter by relaxing the muscles and the former as far as we can by lying on a soft mattress, which distributes the pressure evenly. So, as we keep still, we cease to be disturbed by sensations from our limbs because they have ceased to send us any messages.

Adrian continues:[8]

> The fact that the receptors can be moved about in relation to the external world enlarges their scope enormously. To gain information about an environment there is no need to wait for it to change, for a motile animal can explore a stationary world by changing the relation of the receptors to its environment. Not only does this counteract the rapid adaptation which takes place in many of the receptors, but it enables us to extract information about the external world, not only from proprioceptors—the highly efficient sensory apparatus in the muscles and the joints. In the normal animal, therefore, both rapidly and slowly adapting end organs will co-operate to build up the complete picture of the external world, and the lack of detail in the message from the simple receptors will be filled in by the messages from the complex 'postural' organs that are activated at the same time.

The loss of signals with adaptation is useful in many ways. As Adrian says: 'It might well be inconvenient if our central nervous system were to be continually flooded with messages from every part of the skin surface. . . . The rapid adaptation of the sense organs will make for an absence of monotony and will allow each new sensory excitation to have its full effect on the central nervous system.'[9] Much of this applies to the eyes, which need changes of stimulation to continue signalling to the brain. Local regions of retina become adapted or 'fatigued' with constant stimulation, giving selective loss of signals, and creating the visual 'fictions' of after-images. The ears, however, have remarkably little adaptation with prolonged stimulation; which can be a nuisance as we are often bombarded by irrelevant sounds, which can be extremely annoying.

If a coloured patch, on a similarly bright background, is stared at steadily for several seconds it will gradually disappear, though without leaving much of an after-image. Known as the Troxler Effect, this is not fully explained, but seems to be a cortical rather than a retinal phenomenon (cf Anstis, S. 1967 and 1979).

Lost behind bars

Visual scientists are fascinated by what they call 'spatial frequency channels', by analogy with frequencies in time of sound waves. The visual system is 'tuned' to spatial frequencies of repeated lines, known as *gratings*. (Ideally, the grating bars should not have sharp edges, but should be sine wave modulations of brightness). By varying contrast and spatial frequency (the number of bars per degree of visual angle), they can be used as sophisticated tests of visual acuity. By combining pictures of different special frequencies, or a picture of one spatial frequency on a grating of another frequency, it is possible to create pictures that are seen from some viewing distances but disappear at other

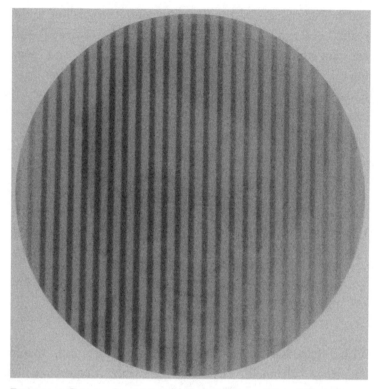

Figure 10. Contrast Sensitivity. Psychologist Fergus Campbell 1924–1993 (from *Psychologists in Word and Image*. Nick Wade (1995), MIT Press).

distances. The psychologist-artist Nicholas Wade has created excellent examples (Figure 10).

There is a beautiful face made of seashells, in the Exploratorium Science Centre in San Francisco. Seen from a distance it is a face; but from nearby it is just a collection of shells. There is a similar effect with any painting having marked brush strokes. From very close one sees only the brush strokes, the picture appearing as one moves further away. This is because the spatial frequencies of the brush strokes and the picture are different. Yet the picture is nothing but brush strokes!

Mind blindness

Loss of vision may occur though there is nothing wrong with the eyes. The problem is in the brain or the mind. But there are various kinds of blindness.

Two kinds of mind blindness were described by the neurologist Heinrich. Lissauer in 1885. He called responding only to stimuli 'apperception', and normal linking of stimuli or sensory data to object-knowledge 'association'. Mind blindness, now called *agnosia*, could be either apperceptive or associative. Some patients show one, and others the other, kind of mind blindness. Some have agnosia only for some kinds of objects; for example, failure to recognize fruits, or animals, or people. The term 'agnosia' was coined by Sigmund Freud when he was a young neurologist.

Inability to recognize faces (*prosopagnosia*) is quite common. There may be no feeling of familiarity, even for close friends. Presumably failure to identify faces is apperceptive, rather than associative loss. Cases of associative agnosia are brilliantly described by Oliver Sacks in several of his books, including *The Man Who Mistook His Wife for a Hat* (1986). Fascinating as human stories, they show most dramatically the importance of available knowledge for seeing.

Neglect, or rejection of sight

Most curious are the strange phenomena of *neglect*, of the left side of the visual field, and sometimes neglect of the left side of the body for touch, with right-hemisphere brain damage. For vision the entire left field may be missing. Oddly, it may be missing as represented with *drawings*, though present to *verbal* description. Most puzzlingly, it may be left halves of objects that are missing, wherever the eyes are looking. The patient may leave the left half of the plate untouched, even though his eyes move freely. This neglect of the left half occurs in drawings from memory, and in copying drawings or objects. For example, the left-hand numbers on a clock face may be omitted, or transferred to the right half of the dial (Figure 11).

This remarkable one-sided neglect can extend to long-term memory. In some experiments patients have been asked to memorize and describe a well-known scene, with the finding that objects on the left are largely omitted. If, however, the patient is asked to imagine the scene from a viewpoint behind it, so that right and left are reversed, then objects that were omitted when they were on the left are now included in the recall, and objects originally on the right are excluded. Perhaps this is not altogether surprising, as it is known from brain imaging that many of the same brain regions are involved in visual memory and seeing.

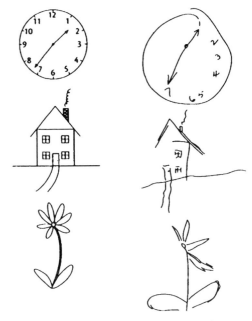

Figure 11. Drawings by left-sided 'neglect' patients having righted-sided stroke. From Robertson and Marshall (1993).[10]

Change blindness

We have hinted at selection, and rejection by *attention*. Although selective attention is extensively investigated, we will not discuss it further here, except for the remarkable phenomenon of blindness to *changes*, as from one picture or scene to another that is somewhat different. This blindness to change, giving continuity, is useful for filmmakers. Although film and television technicians must be aware of this phenomenon, *not seeing change* has only recently been investigated.

There is blindness to change even for quite large differences between two pictures or scenes, especially when the change is not relevant to the task in hand (Figure 12). When the second picture is presented in the same place as the first but following a short gap in time, differences between the pictures may not be seen, though they are obvious when pointed out.

If the pictures are presented in turn with no time-gap, there is a marked motion signal where there is a difference between them, which attracts attention to the change. However, video sequences have been made where, for example, one person replaces another, without the change being noticed.

Why should there be blindness to change? There is lack of agreement among those who have studied this phenomenon, but change blindness is not surprising on the view that perceptions are *predictive hypotheses*. For hypotheses are useful for giving continuity through gaps of data. Of course reliance on running hypotheses does sometimes let one down, but generally only occasional topping-up from fresh data is

Figure 12. Change blindness: look from one picture to the other—are they different? Note the large tree missing to the right of Notre Dame.

needed for continuous perception and continuous behaviour, which is useful.

This reliance on hypotheses of what is out there beyond what is signalled makes conjuring relatively easy. Conjuring shows how fragile perception really is and how far it depends on assuming normal objects doing their usual things. Most conjuring works by the audience seeing what 'should' or would normally happen when the conjuror makes something odd occur. Living by hypotheses can be dangerous.

On this view of change blindness a question to ask is: what normally switches off perceptual hypotheses? As they enrich and fill gaps in sensory data, it is useful to rely on them until there is good evidence that an update is needed. A local movement often signals this; but updating can be spontaneous. An interesting experiment is to view a pair of stereo pictures, one to each eye in a stereoscope. When vivid depth is seen, very gently close one eye. Then the depth continues for quite a while, with only one eye. This must be the depth hypothesis continuing after the 3D evidence is removed. This gives some idea of how long unsupported visual hypotheses continue: for up to about two seconds.

Blindness of cortical functions

The various senses are served by specialized neural systems, in various regions of the outer layers of the cortex of the brain. Vision works with many semi-autonomous systems, gradually being discovered with various techniques. Results of damage are not always easy to interpret though, as weird things can happen to any system when parts are removed. This is very familiar in electronics: removing or damaging a part can upset the functions of other parts in ways extremely hard to predict or sometimes to explain.

It turns out that one processing system may be blind to other kinds of stimuli. Perhaps most striking, the systems for visual movement and stereoscopic depth are colour-blind. They hardly respond to iso-luminant pictures having colour contrast but without brightness contrast. Iso-luminant pictures are unstable, and movement and stereo depth are lost as those brain processes are blind to colour. So, there are many kinds of blindness.

Information theory

When telegraphy and then telephones became commercially important it was necessary to measure information, for information was charged according to speed and reliability. Information is also expensive for nervous systems, so there are economic limits to what can be seen.

So far, no way has been found for measuring meaning. Through information technology, information and meaning have became separated and thought of differently. This affects how we think of the brain and perception and their limitations.

Information is measured in Claude Shannon's mathematical theory of information, by the number of possible choices and their probabilities.[11] A choice between two equally likely probabilities is one *bit*. The bit (binary digit) is the unit of information. Bits add logarithmically, with logarithms to base 2. For an information channel (including a sensory channel), the more closely the output of the channel corresponds to its input, the more information is carried. The channel capacity also depends on the number of bits per second that can be transmitted. The channel capacity for our senses is remarkably low by comparison with electronic channels. Yet, we seem to see a great deal of detail in a short time. This is something of a conundrum, showing value-added brain creativity augmenting signalled information, from object knowledge and with a good deal of fiction.[12]

Information limits

Appreciation of the limited capacity of sensory channels goes back to the Scottish philosopher Sir William Hamilton (1788–1856), who suggested throwing beans on a marble floor and estimating the number of beans. How many could be counted at a glance? The answer is, only about seven. In modern terms, this represents the limited channel capacity of human vision. It is less than it seems to everyday experience. Hamilton's experiment, revealing a surprising low information rate, was interpreted by the Harvard psychologist George Miller with the new concepts of information theory, with a famous paper bearing the memorable title: 'The magic number seven, plus or minus two'.[13] For this is the number of beans, or whatever, that can be seen at one glance. The apparent richness of perception is sometimes called the Great Illusion.

Another revealing experiment was performed by Edmund Hick in 1952, in Cambridge. Hick's apparatus had ten finger-keys, each with a little light placed in a fixed position to the randomly arranged keys. After learning which key belonged to which light, the subject had to press the corresponding key when a light came on as fast as possible. Hick varied the number of keys in a given experimental trial, from one to ten. He found that the response-time increased with the number of lights and keys—that is with the number of choices. This means that lights that *might* come on increased the response time. So, behaviour was not simply from stimuli, but from *possibilities* of stimuli, even when they did not actually happen. This is very different from the old notion that we simply respond to events as they occur, directly to stimuli. For the lights that might come on but don't are not stimuli; yet they affect perception and behaviour and in a systematic way.

We build in our brains mental models that include alternative possibilities. We use sensory signals to select from mental repertoires of possibilities. The larger the repertoire the more the information—requiring more time to process. Edmund Hick found that the time increases to the logarithm (to base 2) of the number of brain-stored possibilities, plus one. He thought of the added *one* as due to the hidden choice of *not* pressing a key.[14]

The physics of neural channels is very different from the wires of telegraphs or telephones, and even more different from radio links; but the underlying principles—limited channel capacity, degeneration of signals by the inevitable random noise, information as choices from a set of possibilities—is the same for electronic and neural channels. Engineering illustrates key concepts for physiology even when there are major differences.

What is knowledge?

We have said that perception is based on knowledge. What is knowledge? How does knowledge relate to information? Knowledge is broader and more structured than information. We might hazard a definition: *knowledge is information structured for use*. It may be implicit, or may be explicit. It may be stored in the genetic code or in brains, and now in computers. Surely artificial intelligence will really take off when computers have rich knowledge of the world they 'live' in. That *perception depends on knowledge* is a central theme of this book.

Notes

1. John Hull, *Touching the Rock* (Preston: Arrow, 1991), 109.
2. R. L. Gregory and G. Wallace, *Recovery from Early Blindness*, Monograph 2, Society of Experimental Psychology (Cambridge: Heffers, 1963).

3. This long delay was because his eyes were in a poor state and doctors did not want to waste precious corneas. When cornea banks were started, it was decided to risk it, and the operations were successful.

4. The children were given upper-case letters engraved on wooden tablets, and they could read them on brass plates and so on. As lower-case letters were not commonly used at that time, the blind school set up the perfect experiment—experience of upper-case but not lower-case letters. Only the already experienced kind of letters could be read by his new-found vision.

5. The investigators are: I. Fine, Alex R. Wade, Alyssa A. Brewer, Daniel F. Goodman, Geoffrey O. Boynton, Brian A. Wandell, and Donald I. A. MacLeod.

6. Elvidina N. Adamson-Macedo, of the University of Wolverhampton in England, finds that neonates have extensive touch exploration and seem to benefit from simple specially designed toys to increase the range of their experience.

7. E. D. Adrian, *The Basis of Sensation* (Cambridge: Cambridge University Press, 1928), 98.

8. Adrian, *The Basis of Sensation*, 100.

9. Ibid., 101.

10. There is a large literature on neglect. See especially Ian H. Robertson and John C. Marshall, *Unilateral Neglect: Clinical and Experimental Studies* (Hove: Lawrence Erlbaum, 1980).

11. Claude Edward Shannon (1916–2001) was an engineer working at the Bell Telephone Laboratories in America. This is a good example of an engineer's solution making a major contribution to solving a philosophical problem.

12. The classic account is the original: Claude E. Shannon and W. Weaver, *The Mathematical Theory of Information* (Urbana, IL: University of Illinois Press, 1949).

13. G. A. Miller (1956), 'The magic number seven plus or minus two: some limits on our capacity to process information', *Psychological Review* 63: 81-97.
14. Edmund Hick and I were the subjects for the original experiment. As he dropped out before completing it, Hick's Law is based on my nervous system.

CONFOUNDED
AMBIGUITY

Seeing depends on contrast. Although of course we can tell day from night, and moonlight looks dim, photographers find it hard to judge the brightness of the light for best exposure, so rely on a meter or trust an automatic camera. The retina signals primarily *differences* of brightness, between one region and another and changes with time. It is spatial differences that give contours for defining objects, and ultimately resolution for seeing details depends on how small are differences of brightness that can be detected.

How small this difference can be depends on many factors, some in eye and brain and others in the scene. Eyes, and *all detectors*, are ultimately limited by random 'noise' disturbance. This can only be reduced by lowering the temperature, which is done for radio telescopes and some medical instruments, but of course human eyes are at blood heat.

The visual brain has to decide whether neural activity is due to the presence of light or to internal neural noise. Both noise and a stream of photons (light) fluctuate randomly. For seeing anything reliably there must be significantly different numbers of photons. They must be statistically *significantly* different. Ability to distinguish something from nothing, or something from another thing, always involves some guessing. For there is always random variation in the rate of photons and changes of neural noise might be mistaken for a genuine signal or stimulus.

Neural noise increases with ageing, so our ability to see and hear and taste degenerates as we get older. Older people may slow down as a strategy to gain time for distinguishing signals from the randomness of their nervous systems, and for reading them as messages from various objects of the external world. This buys reliability at the cost of time (as signals integrate linearly but random noise integrates with a square root function). So driving or walking more slowly is an intelligent adaptation for older people. In dim light the eye becomes more sensitive with dark adaptation, increasing over several minutes, though at the cost of not seeing the precise position of moving objects, as time discrimination is sacrificed. A fast-moving ball may be seen though its exact position may not be noted, as experienced when playing tennis, cricket or baseball in fading light.

In dim light, one can actually see the quantum fluctuation and one's own visual noise. Waking in a dim room, it is interesting to look up at the ceiling, which may seem covered in moving ants. These are spontaneous pulses of visual noise and individual photons, seen in dim light when the eyes are fully dark-adapted.

Similarly one hears sounds in complete silence. It can be unclear whether the sound is out there or created in one's ears. Tinnitus can be a nightmare.

Thresholds

Visual scientists used to talk of sensory '*thresholds*' as though there is a sudden step difference between experiencing nothing or something. We no longer think like this, for sensory thresholds are not sudden or steep but are gradual. They change according to many factors; some in physics, others in physiology or psychology.

Their statistical nature links sensory thresholds with detection by physical instruments and finding important differences by experiments. This was shown in the 1930s for agriculture by the great statistician Sir Ronald Fisher (1890–1962) for assessing the effects of adding fertiliser to a crop of plants. Fisher found he could detect a smaller effect with larger fields, allowing a larger sample of plants. This obeys laws that also hold for eyes detecting photons of light. For eyes are also more sensitive to larger *visual fields*. For, like the plants in the agricultural experiment, some receptors will do slightly better or worse than others and they will vary somewhat in time. This is rather like plants absorbing more or less fertilizer. An increase in number of receptors stimulated will improve the sensitivity of the eye much as larger field sizes improve the sensitivity and reliability in the agricultural experiments. A square root law holds for both. Known as Piper's Law, for vision the threshold brightness

1. Colour contrast: red spirals. How many colours are there?

© Akiyoshi Kitaoka

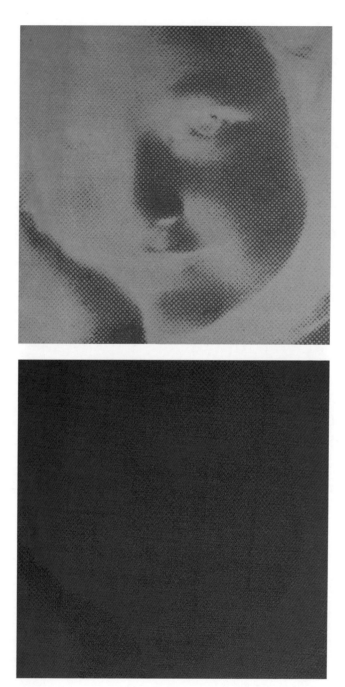

2. Isoluminant face. If viewed through a red or green filter the face is clearly seen.

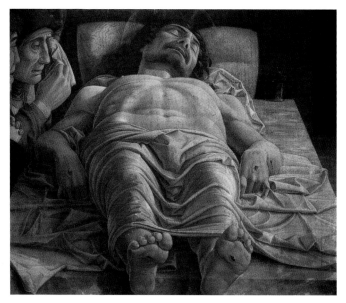

3. *The Lamentation over The Dead Christ* by Andrea Mantegna. This perspective depends on our knowledge of objects – the shape and size of human beings.

© Alfredo Dagli Orti/Galleria Brera, Milan/The Art Archive.

4. Ames Room. The girl is further away than the boy but appears absurdly smaller as we assume the room is rectangular, though it is not.

Susan Schwartzenberg © www.exploratorium.edu

5. *Carte Blanche,* 1965 by René Magritte. We know a horse could not walk with bits missing: this is empirically impossible.

for detection decreases with the square root of the area of the visual field. These laws for seeing differences are basic and suggest a fundamental idea, that seeing is limited by statistical principles. For these laws apply to finding *any* differences, and statistics also allows us to judge the reliability of observations.

Sensitivity of the eyes to different intensities of light increases to the square root of the field sizes, just like Fisher's cornfields. For comparing fields, ideally they should be the same size, as there is a double square root function.[11] These laws must be important for designing legible print. Of course reading is easier in a bright light, as there are more photons, and larger print works like larger fields in Fisher's experiments on plants.

Agricultural fields are often limited by boundaries marked with fences. What sets the boundaries of retinal fields? Except for patches of light surrounded by darkness this is not simple, and objects are seldom isolated. Identifying objects in a stimulus pattern on the retina is a major perceptual feat. It uses every trick in the book. It uses Gestalt laws such as closure (as most objects are simple closed shapes), and common fate (as the parts of most objects move together). Also, top-down knowledge of objects is very important.

What happens to brightness thresholds with borders? In science it is often hard to know which data are relevant and which can be ignored. There must be a similar problem for vision.

Contrast illusions

There are dramatic contrast illusions for brightness and for colour. Figure 13 shows a simple brightness contrast illusion.

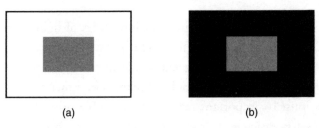

(a)   (b)

Figure 13. Brightness contrast: The inner squares are the same brightness, but appear different.

Shadows

It is remarkable how vision decides between surface reflectance (albedo) and illumination, especially shadow. Shadows tend to be ignored, so the same brightness difference appears greater when it is seen as a reflectance difference of the surface than due to a shadow. This is revealed using *flipping ambiguity* in Figure 14. The squares marked A and B have the same brightness as printed yet look different. This is because one of them is seen as in shadow. This is a matter of probabilities, described with Bayesian statistics (p. 14–16). Painters, unconsciously or not, give clues for a shadow. With their skill they bias the probabilities.

Figure 14. Checkerboard with cylinder casting a shadow. Squares A and B have the same luminance, though they look quite different. Edward H. Adelson (1995).

Colour contrast

Colours are greatly affected by surrounding colours. This can be useful; as for example carpets can be given many colours from only a few pigments (Plate 1).

The same phenomenon can be seen as an illusion or not, depending on whether one is misled. We are surprised by the changes of brightness and colour in the previous figures, but for seeing objects compensations for changes of brightness and colour serve to make things look normal.

Note

1. This was shown by R. L. Gregory and V. R. Cane (1955), 'A statistical information theory of visual thresholds', *Nature* 176: 1272.

FLIPPING AMBIGUITY

There are broadly two theories for why some perceptions flip: that the brain gets tired of one perception, or that there are rival candidates seeking centre stage. Both may be true, but it is interesting that looking for several seconds at a similar figure which does not flip, then at the flipping figure, tends to stabilize it to this alternative (Hohwy, Roepstorff, & Friston 2008). As probabilities are very important, the more cognitive kind of explanation seems appropriate.

Normally a perception changes with a change in what is out there. But remarkably, there can be spontaneous flipping between very different alternative perceptions of an unchanging scene or object. We may say the brain changes its mind as it entertains alternative hypotheses of what is out there.

The most basic perceptual decision is between what are *objects* and what is background between objects. This is known as figure-ground ambiguity. Generally objects are seen right away, but there are situations when the brain cannot make up its mind, and then there is spontaneous flipping as objects essentially disappear, becoming mere ground to emerge after a few seconds as objects.

These are very important phenomena for discovering the dynamics of how perception works. Flipping ambiguity can be used to separate 'bottom-up' sensory signals from 'top-down' brain activity. We will meet this in various places, including distortions of an ambiguous wire cube which we will use for investigating processes of scaling (p. 126)

Figure-ground

The Swedish psychologist Edgar Rubin (1886–1951) brought figure-ground ambiguity to prominence in the early 1920s with examples such as Figure 15.[1]

Rubin described the differences between figure and ground as: 'What is perceived as figure and what is perceived as ground does not have shape in the same way. In a certain sense, the ground has no shape.' Then:

> To characterise the fundamental difference between figure and ground it is useful to consider the contour, which is defined as the common boundary between the two fields. One can then state as a fundamental principle: when two fields have a common border, and one is seen as figure and other as ground, the immediate perceptual experience is characterised by a shaping effect, which emerges from the common border of the fields and

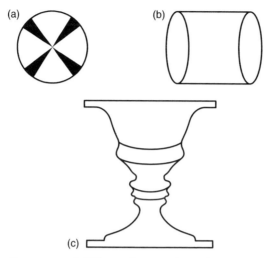

Figure 15. Figure-ground. What is figure—what is background? Above is spontaneous 'flipping' as the brain tries to make up its mind. (After Edgar Rubin).

which operates only on one field, or operates more strongly on one field than the other.

The field which is most affected by this shaping process is *figure*, the other field is *ground*.

Rubin adds:

In relation to the ground, the figure is more impressive, and more dominant. Everything about the figure is remembered better, and the figure brings forth more associations than the ground.

He makes an interesting observation on aesthetics:

The autonomy of the figure relative to the ground has the consequence that, independently of the ground on which it lies, a figure can arouse an aesthetic impression. In contrast, the objective figure which constitutes the ground is usually aesthetically indifferent...worth mentioning as it plays no small rôle in art. When one succeeds in experiencing as figure areas that are intended as ground, one can sometimes see they constitute aesthetically displeasing forms. If one has the misfortune in pictures of the Sistine Madonna to see the background as figure, one will see a remarkable lobster claw grasping Saint Barbara, and another pincer-like instrument seizing the holy sexton. The figures are hardly beautiful.

Attention ('conscious intent') is a factor. Horizontal and vertical features tend to evoke figure. Figure-ground flipping does occur in normal situations though fortunately (as it can be dangerous) it is rare. Studying these phenomena engenders experience of spontaneous flipping.

Flipping objects

An object, or figure, may change spontaneously into something else. Famous, are Rubin's Vase-Faces and Jastrow's Duck-Rabbit. The duck's beak turns into the rabbit's ears. The eye is almost ignored when irrelevant in the duck. This rejection of sensory data when they do not fit the present perceptual hypothesis is part of the dynamics of perception. It can also happen in science, when data seem to be irrelevant or mildly conflicting.

Figure 16. Jastrow's Duck-Rabbit.

Another famous example is E. G. Boring's Young Woman-Old Woman. With a bit of practice, one can make this switch at will—by looking at regions more suggestive of the young or of the old woman.

An eye movement can often initiate a flip, but a physical change is not necessarily needed. The retinal image of a flipping figure can be stabilized as an after-image, by illuminating the figure with an electronic flash in darkness. Although the resulting after-image of an ambiguous figure is completely stabilized on the retina, it will flip spontaneously.

Flipping depth

The most famous figure flipping in depth is the Necker Cube (Figure 17). This was discovered in 1832 by a Swiss crystallog-

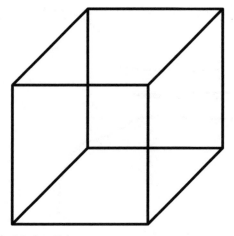

Figure 17. The Necker Cube.

rapher N. A. Necker, while he was drawing rhomboid crystals with a microscope. He was surprised when his drawing suddenly failed to match the crystal in his microscope! One of them had flipped!

Mach's Corner

There are many associated phenomena of great interest. The German physicist Ernst Mach (1839-1916) produced an example of flipping in depth with a related change of sensation—brightness. This is evidence that even basic simple sensations can be modified by top-down modification from the cortex (Figure 18).

When flipped 'in' the grey region is more likely to be a shadow, than when the corner is 'out', when it is more likely to be a mark on the surface. Presumably it appears lighter when seen as

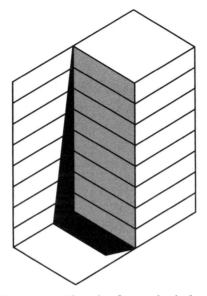

Figure 18. Mach's Corner. When this flips in depth the dark region may change from dark to light.

a shadow, as shadows tend to be visually rejected, because unlike objects they cannot be handled or used. When the corner sticks out, this region is more likely to be its surface. Although there is no physical change it looks darker when 'out' and lighter when 'in', as the probability of it being a surface or shadow changes. This also works for a real corner (say a Christmas card or a menu) with a real shadow.

The Hollow Face

The most dramatic example of probability dominating depth-ambiguity is the Hollow Face (Figure 19). A hollow face mask

Figure 19. The Hollow Face. A hollow mask 'refuses' to appear as hollow, simply because hollow faces are so unlikely.

'refuses' to appear hollow—as a hollow face is so unlikely—unless seen close up with both eyes.

This is a very effective demonstration of the power of top-down knowledge. It dominates bottom-up information from the eyes of texture, perspective, and even quite strong stereoscopic information. It is interesting to look at the Hollow Face closely, with both eyes open, and then walk slowly backwards. It will appear correctly hollow from very close, then flip to convex from slightly further away. Here one is pitting top-down knowledge of normal faces against bottom-up signals for depth clues. At the 'flip-point', bottom-up and top-down balance. The balance point changes if the mask is shown upside down—reversing in depth further away, as the top-down knowledge is weaker for an upside-down hollow face (Hill and Bruce 1993).

Retinal rivalry

When the images in the two eyes are very different, they cannot be 'fused' by the brain. Then we experience dynamic 'rivalry'—changing forms, colours, or whatever. Fused common-contours can lock otherwise rivalling colours. This allows red-green anaglyph stereoscopic pictures to work.

There is evidence that both eyes continue to send signals to the brain during rivalry (they are not inhibited), rivalry being a 'high-level' phenomenon, as later stages of processing try to make sense of the incompatible inputs. There do not seem to be similar phenomena for the ears or for any of the other senses.

Verbal alternation

Other senses can also be dynamically ambiguous. If a word is repeated several times, especially without breaks, it will transform into other words. Alternative perceptions can be changes of stress of rhythm, or accent—or to a different language. This can be done with a tape loop, or on a computer, to make sure the repeated word does not change physically. It works better for some words than others. Good words are 'elephant' and 'sidewalk'. One's own name refuses to flip.[2]

What do 'flipping' phenomena mean?[3]

What makes some objects, or figures or sounds, dynamically ambiguous? Spontaneous flipping increases with practice. It is probable alternatives that tend to be selected.[4] It is as though alternatives, with their relative probabilities, are stored in the brain, waiting in the wings to challenge present perception. After looking at ambiguous figures for several weeks, I found solid objects such as concrete buildings flipping before my eyes. This is disturbing, and no doubt dangerous for driving or flying.

The Austrian philosopher Ludwig Wittgenstein discussed some of these phenomena, asking whether they are changes of perception or of interpretation:[5]

But how is it possible to *see* an object according to an interpretation?—The question represents it as a queer fact, as if something were being forced into a form it did not really fit. But no squeezing, no forcing took place here.

Is there no squeezing or forcing? However this may be, Wittgenstein adds:

And is it really a different impression—in order to answer this I should like to ask myself whether there is really something different in me. But how can I find out?—I *describe* what I am seeing differently.

Here recent brain science comes to the rescue. It is found that brain cells in visual systems fire spontaneously with flips of perception, changing their location. There *were* changes in Wittgenstein's brain. His account reads rather oddly now as at that time seeing and interpreting were thought of as entirely different, though now we may think of interpreting as part of how perception works.

Ambiguity in paintings

Let's look at some principles of perception evident in paintings.

This painting, *Vertumnus*, is typical of Arcimboldo's fruit-faces.[6] It seems to be both fruit and a face. Though impossible for a 'real' object, such ambiguities are important for showing

Figure 20. Arcimboldo's *Vertumnus* (1590 or 1591). Oil on wood. Skoklosters Slott, Balsta, Sweden.

Figure 21. Magritte's road and steeple. The Promenades of Euclid.

Frontispiece.

Whoever makes a DESIGN *without the Knowledge of* PERSPECTIVE *will be liable to such Absurdities as are shewn in this* Frontispiece.

Figure 22. Hogarth's engraving, *The Fisherman.*

how objects seen as perceptions are created from many 'clues' and much knowledge.

Magritte's *The Promenades of Euclid* (Figure 21) has two features with similar shapes, though they appear very different objects.

On the right is a road going off into the distance. On the left is a similar shape but a very different object, a tower with a steeple. This converging shape generally indicates depth by perspective. Renaissance painters learned this for showing depth in pictures, though brains had known it secretly for millions of years.

Here, Magritte is using this depth clue of perspective convergence to represent the road going into the distance, yet the same-shaped steeple looks upright. The *perspective rule* is being countermanded by our *object knowledge* of buildings. It is interesting to mask parts of pictures and see what happens. What happens if the tower is removed?

Hogarth's *The Fisherman* (Figure 22) is the earliest picture known to me of an artist playing with rules of perception to create paradoxes. The longer one looks at it, the weirder it appears. For example, the tramp must be at the same distance as the old lady's candle as they are touching; yet depth clues suggest that he is further away. So he is kind of at the same distance and further. There are other conflicts and ambiguities in the fisherman's line.

This is *perceptual* knowledge; but this can be different from *conceptual* knowledge, so what we see (or hear or touch) may conflict with what we know. For example, when we see a bicycle wheel from an oblique angle it has the appearance of an ellipse: yet we *know* or believe that it is circular. Being circular corresponds to its smooth running (Figure 23).

For a familiar example of conflicting perceptual and conceptual knowledge, an engine driver sees the rails as converging into the

Figure 23. Appearance and reality of bicycle wheels. From a very oblique angle a wheel has the *appearance* of an ellipse though we *know* it is circular. (If it runs smoothly its behaviour confirms it is circular; if it goes bump in the night, we might doubt it!).

distance yet assumes and acts on the belief that they are parallel. Otherwise he wouldn't start the train. He is acting from conceptual knowledge; but this is not always the choice that is made. There is, indeed, a constant battle between perceptual and conceptual reality: sometimes the first, sometimes the second wins. Illusions of perception can produce deceptions of conceptual understanding.

Perception makes somewhat half-hearted efforts to steer appearances towards 'objective' reality. Colour vision takes account of the kind of light, so objects appear almost the same colour, though the light changes. The oblique elliptical wheel is seen as more circular than its retinal image. The rails appear more nearly parallel then they are in the eye.

It is worth noting that the alternative perceptions of flipping ambiguity look equally 'real', yet at least one must be illusory. This means that we are not good at recognizing false from true—for perception or belief.

Notes

1. E. Rubin, *Visuael wahrgenommene Figuren* (Copenhagen: Gyldendalske, 1921).
2. Translated and reprinted in D.C. Beardslee and M. Wertheimer, *Readings in Perception* (Princeton: Van Norstrand, 1958), 194–203.

   The first paper on Verbal Alternation was: R. M. Warren and R. L. Gregory (1958), 'An auditory analogue of the visual reversible figure', *American Journal of Psychology* 71: 612–13.
3. I discuss the significance of ambiguity more fully in *Mind in Science* (London: Weidenfeld & Nicolson, 1981), 383–407.
4. John Harris has found that perspective Necker Cubes, and so on, tend to be seen most often in orientations the perspective indicates. This is neutral in the standard figures. The artist Patrick Hughes uses

reversed-perspective sticking in and out regions of his pictures to give powerful illusions of reversed motion.

5. Ludwig Wittgenstein, *Philosophical Investigations* (1953).

6. Giuseppe Arcimboldo was born in Milan, probably in 1527, ending up as court painter to the Archduke Charles of Austria. He is famous for his faces, made up of other objects—fruits, books etc. He was a superb draughtsman and was highly respected in his own time.

INSTABILITY

Op Art, and all that jazz

Repeated patterns can produce visual 'jazzing'. The artist Bridget Riley made this famous in many of her dramatic Op Art pictures (Figure 24).

There is a current debate on the cause of visual jazzing, and of course there may be more than one cause. The distinguished electro-neurologist Semir Zeki believes that these patterns directly stimulate regions of the brain in cortical area V5, to produce sensations of movement even though there is no movement in the stimuli. Experience of movement without anything moving is not unknown. It applies to the after-effect of movement (p. 167), and to the apparent movement of the Phi phenomenon. So although it may seem unlikely that these particular patterns should stimulate movement systems of the brain, appearance of motion without actual movement can occur. There is, however, an alternative account; that there is motion at the retina from eye tremor, and also hunting of the lens for accommodation, which might stimulate the movement system, especially from high contrast repeated lines or bars.

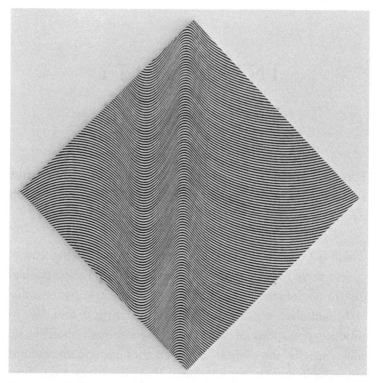

Figure 24. Bridget Riley Op Art.

When the pattern is momentarily stationary on the retina, it produces a brief after-image, which 'beats' with the slightly displaced moving image, giving dynamic Moiré patterns. This principle can be seen by sandwiching a pair of identical overhead transparencies and shifting one across the other. The same chrysanthemum shapes are seen as in the MacKay Rays.[1] It is significant that for the jazzing effect the particular shapes do not matter; what matters is repeated, close-together high contrast lines.[2]

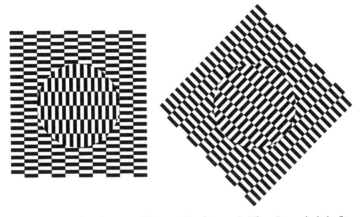

Figure 25. Ouchi illusion. (Hajime Ouchi 1977) The Central disk floats independently to the background.

Remarkable effects are seen with an after-image of one's own hand, viewed in darkness. Illuminate your hand with a bright electronic camera flash, then watch its after-image superimposed on your invisible hand, as you slowly move or rotate it. What happens? Although the retinal after-image is fixed (like a still photograph in one's eyes) it is seen moving—sometimes keeping registered with your moving invisible hand. With a large hand movement it will break away, vision separating from the touch-sensed hand.

Related effects occur if one walks around the after-image of the dark invisible room—it bizarrely becomes rubbery, changing shape as one moves. One is evidently seeing dynamic constancy-scaling, that normally gives stability by compensating changes of retinal images as one moves; but here the compensations create instability, as in the after-image there are no changes to compensate. So we see compensations designed to stop movement as moving!

Illusory table tennis

Donald MacKay noticed, when looking at filaments of valves in a stroboscopically lit room (short flashes of light about 10 times a second), when he moved his eyes the continuously glowing filaments seemed to move around, independently of the glass bulbs they were in.

The effect is dramatic and amusing. If a continuous light (such as an LED) is placed in the middle of a table-tennis bat, illuminated with a stroboscope lamp,[3] the light moves around, even leaving the bat. This curious effect is maximal when the bat is moved unpredictably, by someone else, so the eyes cannot precisely follow its movements. With two such bats, we can play a game of illusory table tennis!

What this effect shows is separation of visual channels for *position* and for *movement*. Normally they agree, without any marked discrepancies; but the stroboscopic flashes fail to activate the *movement* channel, though changes of position are signalled from the continuous light. This creates the curious paradox of change of position without motion. Although physically impossible it can be experienced, showing characteristics of visual channels, free of the physics of objects.[4]

Wobbly pencil

Hold the end of a pencil loosely between two fingers, and oscillate the hand up and down rapidly. Especially in dim light, the pencil will seem to be made of rubber. Is this, also, separation of movement from position signals? The dim light increases signalling delay, associated with dark adaptation. Possibly the position channel is more affected than the movement channel by this increase in delay.

Wobbly windmill

It is interesting to look from quite close, at the rotating blades of a giant wind generator producing electricity on a wind-farm. Seen from an oblique angle (about 10° from normal) the blades seem to bend, as though made of rubber. This is particularly odd, as this is a massive rigid rotating structure.

The ends of the long narrow blades have constant velocity to the eyes when viewed normally; but from an oblique angle, the velocity of each blade at the retina increases and decreases, from around vertical to around horizontal, signalling a change of speed at the eyes, though with *knowledge* that they have a constant angular rotation. The knowledge may maintain rigidity against changes of the velocity signals; or these may beat the knowledge into submission, according to which is stronger.

Retinal rivalry

The two eyes, working together, give stereoscopic depth when there are small horizontal differences between 'corresponding points' in the eyes' images. As the eyes are separated horizontally, their images are from slightly different viewpoints.

Try looking at a vertical pencil, with one eye open, then with the other eye open. It will appear to shift, against more distant objects. The difference between the eyes' images is greater the closer the nearer object. The horizontal difference ('disparity') is used by the visual brain to signal stereoscopic depth. 3D pictures work by presenting the same disparities in a pair of pictures, presented one to each eye, with a stereoscope of some kind. The pictures may be routed to each eye with red-green glasses. When the pictures are 'fused' they appear dramatically in 3D depth.[5]

There is a limit to the disparity that can be fused by the brain. Known as 'Parnam's Limit', this is about 1 degree subtended angle. The brain fails to combine images with differences greater than this limit. Then, we generally see slow dynamic 'rivalry' as one eye and then the other rejects, and then accepts and combines various parts of their visual fields. This dynamic, slowly changing effect is quite unpleasant.

Retinal rivalry also occurs when the eyes are given different brightnesses, or different colours. It is indeed surprising that the red-green glasses used for 3D cinema (anaglyphs) work so well. Remarkably, they do not produce rivalry from the colour difference when there are corresponding features of the two pictures fused by the brain. Try looking at a white wall with the red-green glasses—there will be ever-changing patches of unfused colours. Then look at shared contours, and rivalry will cease. Just why fused contours prevent colour rivalry is unknown. Extreme brightness contrasts, such as white lines to one eye and the same lines but black to the other eye (or photographic positive and negative pictures in a stereoscope) will not fuse, and will hardly give 3D vision. Rivalry occurs when the combined images do not make sense.

Lustre

A shiny surface of polished metal has a dynamic lustre due to retinal rivalry. Unlike a matt surface, local regions of brightness change a lot with a small change of viewing angle. The brightness differences at the eyes are in places too different for fusion. Gold leaf gets its lively lustre largely by retinal rivalry from local brightness differences, so with a single eye it looks lacklustre.

Isoluminance

There are remarkable losses of visual perception when there is *colour* contrast but no *brightness* contrast. This is known as isoluminance. (Or, to avoid mixing Latin with Greek, equiluminance). With only colour contrast edges appear unstable, letters are hard to read, faces composed of red and green dots of equal brightness fail to look like faces. This is remarkable as almost anything looks like a face! Also, movement is almost completely abolished, and Julesz random dot stereo disappears. Depth is generally impaired.[6]

There is, also, loss of the Café Wall distortion illusion (Figure 31). We may guess that this might be associated with 'border locking'. As vision works with many parallel channels—signalling position, movement, stereo depth, and so on separately—there must be a problem of *registration*. This problem is obvious in colour printing.

With isoluminance there is loss of form perception, of movement, and especially of stereo depth. There is extensive research on the physiological bases of these dramatic perceptual losses, when there are no brightness but only colour differences. As colour vision in mammals is only present in primates, it seems to be a late evolutionary development tacked on to much older form perception, like painting by numbers. Underlying physiology has recently been investigated in detail.[7]

Moving experiences

It is remarkable that the brain's 'virtual reality' of the world of objects, conjured from retinal images and object knowledge, is usually so stable. But there are situations when stationary objects move. A perhaps too familiar example is the unsteadiness associated with liberal alcohol. This loss of stability may be related to the 'auto-kinetic effect'.

The auto-kinetic effect

When a small dim light is observed for several minutes in a dark room, it seems to swing around, generally in a fairly random path. If, however, the eyes are held hard to one side, and then centred, there is marked apparent movement in one, usually the opposite direction, lasting for several seconds.

It is often thought that the auto-kinetic effect is due to the eyes moving; but this is not so, though it is related to the eye-movement system. It can be shown with a simple apparatus that auto-kinetic movement occurs though the eyes are stationary.[8]

What is happening? Normally the world remains stable while the eyes are moving. This is different from a panning ciné or video camera, when the world swings round in the opposite direction. It is also different from pushing an eye gently with a finger, when again the world swings around. Normally with voluntary eye movements, motion of the retinal image on the moving retinas is cancelled by the equal and opposite signals from commands to rotate the eyes.[9] What happens can be teased out with some simple-to-do observations:

(1) Try moving the eyes—the surrounding scene remains stable.
(2) Try pushing an eye (the other shut) gently with a finger— the scene moves.

Now try these with an *after-image*, in total darkness.
For (1) The after-image moves, with the eyes.
For (2) There is no movement of the after-image.

These observations reveal a beautiful system that normally keeps the world from spinning around. But such a cancelling system is sensitive to any small imbalance. The auto-kinetic effect is almost certainly due to slight fluctuations of the eye muscles, giving command signals *to keep the eyes still*. Holding them over hard to one side fatigues one set of muscles producing imbalance of the system, so requiring correction—giving a maintained correction command in the opposite direction-seen as movement.

Why doesn't the scene around us normally swing around, randomly, as for the little light in darkness in the auto-kinetic effect? In other words, why don't we get the auto-kinetic effect all the time? Presumably the assumption of a stable world needs strong signals to overcome it. Holding the eyes hard in one direction can make the world swing round as for the little light, though far less, as assumption of a stable world is strong. We are biased against seeing earthquakes, and they are extremely frightening as basic assumptions are disturbed.

Experiencing the world swinging around one—as sitting inside a rotating drum—is sick-making. It is always a question: What is moving—oneself, or surrounding objects?[10]

Induced movement

A familiar experience is seeing the stationary train we are sitting in apparently moving when the neighbouring train moves off. All movements are relative. Here, the wrong choice is made. It turns out that *smaller* objects are generally seen as moving. There is a general assumption—usually true—that the whole scene is fixed while smaller objects move relative to it.

A related illusion occurs when a large background is moved—smaller and nearer objects being seen to move in the opposite direction. This 'induced movement' reflects the brain's assessment of probabilities of what is moving and what is still. Smaller, nearer objects generally move against larger, more distant-fixed backgrounds.

Only accelerations can be signalled by the otolyths of the inner ear. Steady movements need a guessing game to see what is happening. As we have evolved with our feet on the ground, informing us whether and how we are moving, we are surprisingly good at seeing what is moving and where while we are carried along with our feet off the ground, as in a car. Birds solve the problem wonderfully well. It is a dangerous illusion for pilots.

Moving staircase effect

A moving staircase is surprising, as stairs generally do not move, as are the long horizontal travellators at airports, which are great for experiments on dissociating visual and proprioceptive movement while walking. For people familiar with them, there is a remarkable sensation when stepping on to a *stationary* moving staircase. It is easy to stumble, as its usual movement is anticipated though not present.[11] This shows that specific anticipations can be learned rapidly.

Motion parallax

As we move sideways (or up and down) the world swings visually in the opposite direction, around the point to which the eyes are converged. Try moving your head from side to side while looking at a near object, then at a middle distance, then at a far object. Everything rotates in the opposite direction around the object you are looking at. It is interesting to try this for the scenery on a train journey.

This relative motion of near and far is optical.[12] Motion parallax can signal distance quite accurately, and it has been suggested that the neural mechanisms for this are the evolutionary origin of the brain's ability to see stereoscopic depth from the slightly different images of the two eyes, giving simultaneous parallax information.[13]

Depth-reversed parallax

When depth is perceptually reversed (as when a wire cube, or the Hollow Face is depth-reversed) the object appears to rotate in the reversed direction. It follows the viewer's movements—at twice the speed. This is because as near and far are perceptually reversed, although the parallax is physically unchanged, *distant* features are seen as *near* features, giving reversed rotation. This bizarre effect is well worth trying with a wire cube (p. 184).

Pseudo-parallax

Strange things happen when distances are represented on the flat surfaces of pictures. As one moves around the picture, there 'should' be parallax shifts between near and far; but although the picture may appear in quite realistic depth, there are no such changes at the retina. So one might think that nothing will happen—but this is wrong. With convincing, though illusory, picture depth, we see the opposite of what happens with true depth. A picture with marked depth swings around to follow one as one moves around it. The more realistic the depth, the more powerful, is this pseudo-parallax movement. This is a perceptual, not a physical, effect. It is not directly driven by the picture stimulus. If we rotate the picture rather than move ourselves, generally nothing happens—though any change of the picture image in the eye is identical. Normally, a near object keeps the same retinal image when it moves (rotates) to keep facing the viewer. Evidently we attribute this rotation to the picture.

As this works for apparent depth whatever the object shown, it evidently can be *rule*-based (which is where it appears in the Peeriodic Table, p. 242). As one is moving and the eyes keep aimed at one, they must if real eyes be rotating to follow one's movement. This is what we see so dramatically in the portrait. This was noticed by Ernst Gombrich.[14]

Depth seen in stereo pictures, including Julesz' random dot 3D pictures, where there are no objects, show this effect. This depends on stereo depth being *seen*—disappearing when stereo depth is lost, so evidently it is not driven directly from stereo disparity, and does not depend on knowledge of objects (such as eyes).

Illusory movement in real scenes

Looking down from a tall building or a bridge over a deep ravine, objects below seem much too small, and they move *with* instead of against the viewer's movements.

This is related to size constancy. Size constancy fails from unusual heights. It seems that steeplejacks, and builders of skyscrapers, do have symmetrical size-scaling for objects above and below them, so presumably they do not get this effect. It depends on distances being seen incorrectly (when objects look too small or too large) and is associated with size constancy and its errors.

Seeing a stable world though we are moving, evidently requires elaborate compensations, which can go wrong in characteristic ways. It is interesting to compare passive (being wheeled around) movement with active observer motion. It is also interesting to compare effects of familiar with unfamiliar environments. We still have a lot to learn here.

OHO faces and upside-down writing

Perception of faces has many intriguing phenomena. Faces are seen with absurdly minimal cues—hence the Man-in-the-Moon, and the face seen from orbiting satellites in a rock pattern on Mars. Perceptual face-creation at the drop of a hat is a boon to cartoonists. Intriguing are OHO faces, which change from one face to another when inverted. Whistler created many excellent examples (Figure 26). This works because faces are usually 'right way up' with the mouth below the eyes. When inverted, the features are given different probabilities of being a nose, a mouth and so on, simply because a mouth is normally below a nose.

Writing can work similarly. Scott Kim produced wonderful examples of writing (including my name) that remains the same when inverted (fig. 27).

The Thatcher illusion

A perhaps related effect is the Thatcher illusion discovered by the English psychologist Peter Thompson (Figure 28). The smiling mouth is cut out and inverted. Now the face looks bizarre. But when this whole face is inverted one hardly notices the mouth as unusual. This suggests that each facial feature

Figure 26. OHO faces. Try turning the book upside down.

Richard
L.
Gregory

Figure 27. OHO writing. Try turning the book upside down.

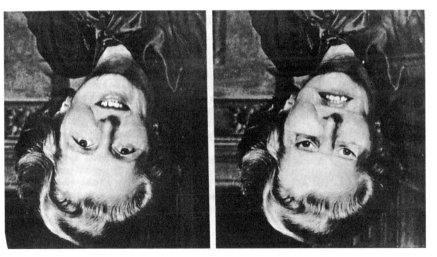

Figure 28. The Thatcher illusion. The mouth is cut out and inverted. Try rotating the whole picture. The weird effect disappears.

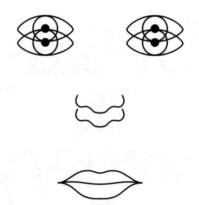

Figure 29. Displaced eyes. This curious jazzing shows the importance of seeing eyes.

receives special processing. This amazing effect suggests that face perception is rather special, and 'wholistic'. It is attributed to processing in the fusiform 'face area' of the cerebral cortex.

Lastly, if the eyes in a picture are duplicated, so that one pair is set slightly below or above the other eyes, there is a quite dramatic jazzing effect. It would be interesting to record the viewer's eye movements. Are they correcting errors that are not there? This works especially well for eyes (Figure 29).

Notes

1. The jazzing is reduced when looking at the figures through a pin-hole, surely because the fluctuations in accommodation then have little or no effect, and are removed when viewed perfectly stabilized on the retina as a flash after-image. (R. L. Gregory (1995), 'Brain-created

visual motion: an illusion?' *Proceedings of the Royal Society of London* B 260: 167–8).

2. Evidence is given in these papers, though this is controversial: R. L. Gregory (1993), 'A comment: MacKay Ray's shimmer due to accommodation changes', *Proceedings of the Royal Society of London* B, 253: 123; Gregory (1995), 'Brain-created visual motion'.

3. The LED should be in a hole in the centre of the bat, which is covered with translucent white paper. When illuminated with a not too bright stroboscope, set to about 7–10 flashes/second, the continuously illuminated hole will move around the bat—even leaving it altogether—looking like a table tennis ball.

4. Continual movements of the lens hunting for focus, or accommodation, impairs seeing into eyes with an ophthalmoscope. It is now possible to compensate this disturbance with a technique developed for astronomy—Active Optics—to minimize degeneration of telescope images through the turbulent atmosphere. A computer-controlled flexible mirror is distorted to compensate the disturbances. This works so well for looking into the eye, that individual receptors (rods and cones) can be seen in the living human eye. This should help diagnosis of retinal degeneration, as with diabetes. By monitoring the correcting signals, it is possible to measure dynamic astigmatism of its wobbly lens. It is also possible to use the system backwards—for stimulating very small regions of the retina, even down to single receptors (Miller et al. 1996). Could the much simpler sampling of lucky imaging be used to see into eyes?

5. The English physicist Sir Charles Wheatstone discovered stereo vision and invented the stereoscope just before photography, in 1832, first published in 1838. See N. J. Wade, *Brewster and Wheatstone on Vision* (London: Academic Press, 1983).

6. R. L. Gregory (1977), 'Vision with isoluminant colour contrast: 1. A projection technique and observations'. *Perception* 6.1: 113-19; V. S. Ramachandran and R. L. Gregory (1978), 'Does colour provide an input to human motion perception?' *Nature* 275: 55–6.

7. M. S. Livingstone and D. H. Hubel (1984), 'Anatomy and physiology of a colour system in the primary visual cortex', *Journal of Neuroscience* 4: 309–56.

8. The centre of the retina (the *fovea centralis*) is almost blind to blue light. (There are individual differences.) One can see the movements in the dark of one's own eyes (or lack of movement) by fixating a small blue light. When fixated, it disappears. By surrounding it with a dim red ring of light it can be fixated, and any eye movement gives a flash of blue. It is found that the auto-kinetic effect continues while the eyes are still. R. L. Gregory (1959), 'A blue filter technique for detecting eye movements during the autokinetic effect', *Quarterly Journal of Experimental Psychology* 11: 113.

9. This works faster—with zero delay—than feedback from the eye muscles, though this is used as a secondary system for a rough eye-position sense.

10. There is no surprise with voluntary eye movements.

11. Moving staircases are poorly designed for stereoscopic vision. It is easy for the eyes to fixate different parallel lines, giving the 'wallpaper illusion', which could be dangerous (cf. p. 16).

12. The same effect is used by astronomers to measure the distances of the nearest stars, using twice the distance of the Sun (186,000,000 miles) as the base line, by taking photographs at six-month intervals.

13. This is suggested by Brian Rogers, at Oxford, who has produced observer-shifted simulated parallax on a computer screen, showing illusory depth; cf. I. P. Howard and B. J. Rogers, *Seeing in Depth*, 2 vols (Oxford: Oxford University Press, 2002).

14. E. H. Gombrich, *Illusion in Nature and Art* (London: Duckworth, 1960), ch. 8.

DISTORTION

There are many kinds of visual distortions. Again, we may class some as phenomena of *reception* and others of *perception*. The first is from disturbed sensory signals, the second from misreading signals or data. Although this distinction seems clear, in practice it is hard to classify some distortion phenomena and there are long-standing debates. This is a complicated business, which we will discuss quite fully with some controversial ideas.

One might say the distinction between *disturbed* and *misread* signals is the distinction between physiology and psychology—the hyphen in physiological-psychology. Though at least to my mind this is basic, it is controversial.[1] As a help to thinking about it, the distinction applies in a now familiar way to computers. When a computer 'hangs up', the trouble may be a *hardware* failure or very differently a *software* error. The 'treatments' are different for hardware and software computer errors, with life-death clinical decisions for medicine.

When something is said to be 'distorted' we should ask, 'Distorted from what?' There must be some accepted, non-distorted reference, for 'distorted' to have meaning. Indeed this applies to any illusion. There must be reference truth for 'illusion' to have meaning. Changes of accepted truth change claims of what is illusory.

Signal errors

We have suggested that some distortions are due to errors of neural signals, others to misreading signals or data. As the first kind of distortions are 'owned' by physiologists and the second by psychologists, there can be professional rivalry for who owns illusions! We will try to decide, using several examples, but colleagues will not all agree. These debates inspire questions and may suggest new experiments.

IRRADIATION

A white square looks slightly larger than a black square of the same physical size. In general, a dividing line between a light and a dark region is displaced towards the dark. Although a small effect, this is important for astronomical observations.

Irradiation is not as simple as it may seem. A very small, dark object such as a telephone wire looks *larger* against a bright sky. Writing and printed letters are usually black with a white background, as also for (Snellen) charts for eye tests assessing visual acuity, so eyes work well with black on white.

In a recent paper the American expert on vision Gerald Westheimer (Westheimer 2007) attributes shift into the dark to the optics of images and to non-linearity of retinal illumination and sensation of brightness.

Light is generally modified in various ways before it reaches the eye. From objects in the heavens there is a large delay depending on the distance: eight minutes for the sun, two million years for the Andromeda nebula (the most distant object visible to the naked eye) and billions of years for the most distant telescopic objects. This means, of course, that astronomers spend their professional lives in the past, confronting objects that no longer exist. This time-travel makes it possible to see the evolution of the universe.

The seventeenth-century optical inventions of telescopes and microscopes were initially distrusted, as it was common knowledge that curved glass distorted. Yet, by enlarging retinal images, they transformed astronomy and biology. Galileo demonstrated the reliability of telescopes by predicting which ships just visible on the horizon belonged to awaiting merchants; but it stretched the reach of experiments to verify new claims for science, based on this extended vision. Famously Galileo was unable to see the rings of Saturn as rings encircling the planet, evidently because this was so unlikely, from his experience of earthly objects. As interpreting sensory signals depends on what is likely from everyday experience, Saturn's rings, being quite outside experience, had zero probability and so were effectively invisible.

Early telescopic observations gradually introducing new ideas, challenged accepted beliefs and created theological controversy. The pock-marked blemished moon challenged heavenly perfection; the earth-centred solar system was mocked by the toy solar system of Jupiter's moons. They were hard to deny, yet for many even harder to accept as science changed how the world was seen and understood, and radically changed behaviour with its technologies.

Telescopes and microscopes from the seventeenth century revealed entirely unknown structures and objects to vision, that could not be experienced by any of the other senses—so giving the eyes special status. No wonder gifted people were called 'bright'! Yet, a far older optical instrument separated vision from the other senses—mirrors. The mirror world is indeed the opposite of blindness—touch without sight. And the mirror world is separated from the combined touch-sight world of everyday experience—being through the mirror. Light is much stranger than envisaged by the philosophers. And mirrors were important in mythologies, as windows to worlds beyond death.

The *virtual images* of mirrors were mysterious, existing only when seen, (or more precisely only when imaged by the eye, or convex lenses or concave mirrors). Virtual images of flat mirrors are like Bishop Berkeley's notion that objects exist only when seen; and this kind of concept has also recently arisen in quantum physics. Yet, as Newton clearly described in his *Optics* of 1704, the virtual images of plane mirrors depend on imaging by eyes, or indeed by cameras. Reflected objects are assumed by the visual system to lie along lines of sight—so when the light is bent their positions are mis-seen. Seeing in a mirror is curiously paradoxical, as the reflected world separates from the world of objects directly seen and touched, giving two perceptual realities for each object, including oneself. It is remarkable that we see ourselves *through* the looking-glass yet know we are in front of it. This mirror distortion of distance is entirely different from the right-left mirror reversal, being optical, and readily understood from a ray diagram. It is simply due to the light path from object to eyes via the mirror being longer than when the object is seen directly. The visual system of eye and brain knows nothing of the mirror, only that the object is optically more distant than its physical position.

RIGHT-LEFT MIRROR REVERSAL

The physics of light reflected from mirrors, as we understand it, is not at all like the ancient analogy of balls bouncing from walls. According to the recent theory of Quantum Electrodynamics (QED), photons do not bounce off reflecting surfaces, but are absorbed and re-emitted from atoms of the surface layers (Feynman 1985). The well-known law of reflection: 'The angle of reflection equals the angle of incidence' is explained statistically, as light reflects at all angles, though predominantly at the angle it strikes the mirror. QED explains why light seems to choose where it strikes the mirror to take the least-time path, so that the angles of incidence and reflection are equal. This is totally different from Greek physics, and just as different from what seems obvious to our common sense. The weird 'distorting mirrors' of fun fairs, are less puzzling than the familiar looking-glass, giving right-left though not up-down reversed images. How does the looking-glass treat vertical and horizontal differently though it is symmetrical? How can a flat piece of glass know right from left? The reason why is not shown in Newton's diagram, or indeed in any optical ray diagram.

What is happening is most easily seen with written or printed letters, as their reversals are immediately recognized. The capital letters A, M, U, V, T are unchanged, yet E, F, K, L, P look different in the mirror—horizontally reversed—as they are not horizontally symmetrical. So the mirror effect is obvious for the second set of letters though not for the first set. Why mirror reversal is right-left yet not up-down has been a question of controversy for hundreds, indeed thousands of years. I discuss it in *Mirrors in Mind* (1997), and most recently in 'Shaving in a mirror with Ockham's razor' (Gregory 2007). There has been, and indeed still is, a remarkable variety of accounts, the philosopher Immanuel Kant even concluding that that this is a problem too difficult for the human mind to grasp.

We may see the answer as simple though the question is puzzling. It may be hard to see what *kind* of problem this is. Is it a matter of physics or optics, of our anatomy or brain organization, of psychology or logic, or of language? All have been called upon for explanation. There are too many tempting though misleading possibilities, and nonsense continues to be written, even in respected scientific journals.

It has nothing to do with the roughly horizontal symmetry of the human form; or the horizontal separation of our eyes; or the reversal of light in the eyes (symmetrical in all directions); or with cross-connections of the right and left halves of the brain (why should only mirror images be reversed, and not all seen objects?) The words 'right' and 'left' can indeed be ambiguous, as for stage directions; but how could ambiguity of language possibly give consistent visual reversal? 'Mental rotation' is a plausible psychological candidate, but it is painfully slow and inaccurate, while mirror reversal is immediate and precise. A helpful clue: a *photograph* taken in a mirror is reversed identically, yet a camera does not have brain or mind, or language!

So, why *are* mirror images reversed sideways yet not up-down? What is interesting is why, for almost everyone, this is such a puzzling question. If this is puzzling, what hope do we have for understanding a puzzle such as consciousness?

Here is a clue from a little experiment worth trying: writing on a transparent sheet reflected in a mirror may *not* be reversed. It is only seen as 'mirror-writing' when it is *rotated* around its vertical axis, to face the mirror. Writing on a transparent sheet does not need to be rotated, to be seen in the mirror— though an opaque sheet of writing or a book does need to be rotated, from direct view, to be visible in the mirror behind it.

Mirror reversal is given by rotation of objects, from direct view, to face the mirror. Objects are generally rotated around their vertical axis, because of gravity; but an object can be rotated around its *horizontal* axis to face the mirror. Then it appears (as it is) upside down, and not right-left reversed.

One sees the object, or the writing, as it has been rotated from direct view, to be seen in the mirror. This applies to oneself: If one stands on one's head to see oneself in the mirror one is not reversed right-left, but is upside-down. There is a complexity though, for there is a little-understood perceptual correction to inverting the head. (Try tilting the head: the world remains upright, quite different from a camera.) Experimenting with mirrors is well worthwhile.[2]

What about very large objects—a scene with mountains and so on—reflected in a mirror? How can a whole scene be rotated? It isn't. There is another rotation that can do the trick— *rotation of one's eyes*—to see the mountains or whatever is behind one in the mirror in front.

In the driving-mirror of a car one sees backwards while looking forwards. The head is turned around from direct view of the scene behind to look into the mirror in front. Here, the mirror reversal is given by rotation of the head and eyes.

Mirror-reversal is due to one or other of these rotations from direct view: rotation of objects, or of the eyes. When this is not recognized, there is a mysterious puzzle. But—unlike optical or perceptual illusions—this disappears when it is understood.

It is a fine line between illusions of seeing and delusions of thinking. Mirror reversal is very simple physics, but like conjuring, looks mysterious when not understood. If only philosophy and education could resolve other puzzles so neatly!

ADAPTATION

Vision is changed by what we look at, and by prevailing conditions, such as brightness of the light. The eye loses its sensitivity in bright light, and it gradually recovers sensitivity during 'dark adaptation', taking nearly an hour to complete though initial adaptation is rapid. Staring at curved lines will make straight lines briefly appear distorted the opposite way (Figure 30).

Adapting to patterns or objects may be due to loss of neural function as neural components become 'tired' or the visual system may be recalibrated. It can be uncertain whether visual adaptation is a design failure or is useful-designed by natural selection to improve efficiency, and so chances of survival.

These phenomena may be used to tease out and discover neural channels, that signal tilt or curvature spatial frequency or whatever, including colours. However, effects of adaptation seldom relate appearances to underlying physiology in a simple way; for appearances generally depend on many neural systems contributing in various ways. For example, although it is believed that *tilt* is signalled by specific channels, special channels for *curvature* have not been found, and curves are probably signalled by many tilt channels combined. This seems more

 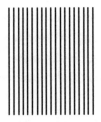

Figure 30. Adapting to tilt, to curves, to spatial frequencies. Stare at the curved lines for about 10 seconds, then look at the vertical lines. They 'should' curve the other way, briefly. After staring at the curves, the straight lines 'should' appear curved the other way.

likely, as there are so many curves there could hardly be a special channel for each.

This seems more like colour adaptation, where the balance of three overlapping channels is disturbed when a colour is stared at for several seconds. Specific colours do not have specific channels. All colours are signalled as mixtures from three channels, responding to long, medium, or short wavelength light. There are very few simple correlations between physiology and phenomenal phenomena—so we generally have to think with quite complicated models for how the physiology might work.

Returning then to our earlier question: do phenomena of adaptation show design weaknesses of the nervous system, or do adaptation changes serve the useful purpose of recalibrating the systems to avoid errors in the longer term? Either can occur. After-images are due to local regions of retinal fatigue, giving temporary brightness and colour reversal; as children's eyes grow further apart the baseline for their stereoscopic depth increases, but as this is somehow compensated for, so seen distances are unchanged.[3] More generally, it seems that vision is checked by touch, and vice versa; so vision and touch generally agree and help each other. But this is easily upset. If you run your finger around the circular top of a wine glass, while watching it with a distorting (astigmatic) lens, the glass comes to feel distorted. All the senses are labile, and affect each other, generally keeping them in agreement.

When, however, a neural channel becomes adapted though other parallel channels are unaffected, various things can happen. The odd-man-out may be rejected, or may be combined with channels signalling differently, producing *paradox*. The philosopher George Berkeley, as we saw, considered placing one hand in hot water and the other in cold, then placing both hands in tepid water. He found it feels cold and hot at the same time. With after-effect of movement, movement is seen though with no change of position. For the movement channel adapts but the position channel is unaffected, so they conflict, with a physical impossibility.

A CROSS-CHANNEL ADVENTURE—THE CAFÉ WALL ILLUSION

A striking, readily investigated distortion illusion, is the Café Wall. Named from the pattern of tiles on a nineteenth-century café in Bristol, it is like a chessboard, except that the rows of tiles are separated by narrow grey 'mortar lines', and alternate rows are displaced by half a tile width. Strangely, although the mortar lines are parallel they appear as long

Figure 31. The Café Wall. The alternate convergence of the wedges is illusory. There are only parallel lines, and right angles in this figure. This illusion figure can be varied in a number of ways, what happens being remarkably lawful and easy to measure.

wedges[4] (Figure 31). The effect is so strong it is hard to believe they are indeed parallel.

The wedge distortions are challenging, as they seem to violate a principle of physics—Curie's Principle, which states that systematic asymmetry cannot be produced from symmetry.[5] Yet, the illusory wedges are asymmetrical though the figure is symmetrical. For the pattern of tiles repeats along the rows, so has symmetry, as one region is exactly the same as others along the row. How can this symmetrical pattern produce the asymmetrical wedge distortion? This requires two stages, the first being local asymmetry (which is no problem). Each pair of light-dark tiles is asymmetrical. These produce small wedge distortions, which by a second process of extrapolation, produce the long wedges. The little local wedges are not obvious when they form the long wedges, but are seen when there are much smaller tiles. Presumably they fail to integrate into long wedges, as the local distortion is too steep.

By varying features of this figure, several Laws of the Café Wall emerge:

Laws of the Café Wall:

1. The alternate wedge distortions reverse when, and only when, alternate rows are shifted by half a cycle.
2. The mortar must subtend less than 10 minutes of arc. The distortion is greatest with narrow mortar lines.
3. The distortion is maximal when the mortar luminance is mid-way between the luminances of the tiles—being zero when the mortar is darker than the dark tiles or lighter than the light tiles.
4. The distortion increases, with increase in luminance contrast of the tiles.
5. The distortion is zero with colour contrast, but *no* brightness contrast—isoluminant tiles.
6. With many small tiles, the long wedge distortion is replaced by many short wedges.

7. The distortion increases when the retinal image is blurred, as by screwing up the eyes.

The Café Wall has no depth clues. There is no perspective, as there are only parallels and right angles. (The illusory wedges can, however, appear as rotated in depth, from their illusory perspective shapes. But here the distortion produces the (occasional) appearance of depth, rather than depth clues producing distortion.)

The complicated distortions of the Café Wall can be isolated in a simple effect, so strange that we call it the 'Phenomenal Phenomenon'.[6]

THE PHENOMENAL PHENOMENON

The 'Phenomenal Phenomenon' is what happens to a gray rectangle with a narrow light border on one of its long edges, and a narrow dark border on the opposite edge (Figure 32). When its (or its background) illumination is changed,[7] it appears to *move* dramatically. The light border of the rectangle *leads*, as its illumination *increases*, and vice versa with increase of the background luminance. Dramatic movement is seen while the illumination is changing; with a static shift, when rectangle and background have a fixed brightness difference.

If we add a second rectangle—identical, except that its light and dark narrow edges are mirror-reversed—they move in opposite directions. Using a stereoscope—so one eye sees one of the

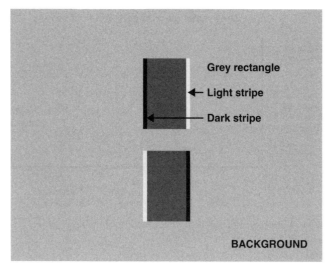

Figure 32. Stereo Phenomenal Phenomena—of movement, position, depth. The grey rectangles, with their narrow light and dark edges, move dramatically when made brighter or darker than the background. They move in opposite directions, the borders are mirror-reversed—giving stereo depth when viewed one to each eye. This figure shows the 'Phenomenal' movement, position, and stereo depth. All three functions are all different.

rectangles and the other eye the mirror-reversed rectangle—they move nearer and further in *depth*, from their opposed sideways shifts. The illusory motion and the static shift affect the stereoscopic system as though they are real.

What happens in detail is quite surprising. When we compared the illusory changes of *position, velocity,* and of *stereo depth*, it turned out that all three are different functions, plotted in (Figure 33).

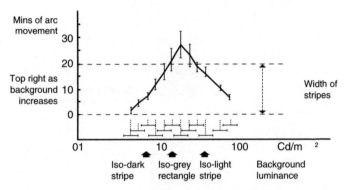

Figure 33. Graph for Phenomenal Phenomenon, showing position, velocity, and stereo depth.

The full story is quite complicated. All three functions are different, presumably showing the neural channels have different characteristics.[8]

The 'Phenomenal Phenomenon' seems to be the basis of the Café Wall wedges illusion. This is affected similarly by brightness changes of the 'mortar' lines, the illusory movements of the 'tiles' with changing brightness of the 'mortar lines' being truly dramatic.

BORDER-LOCKING?

We have suggested, as a speculation, that these phenomena reveal a normally hidden though important process, that we may call *border-locking*. As vision works with many parallel channels, it seems quite wonderful that neighbouring bright and dim regions of a moving object all move together, neatly registered at borders; even though channels have greater delay in dim light and colours have different delays.

For colour printing, it is difficult to keep borders of colour and luminance in registration, and colours are apt to 'bleed'; yet the eye hardly ever suffers such discrepancies, even for moving objects or patterns.

We know there are different delays from physiological record-ing, and from the astonishing Pulfrich Pendulum phenomenon (p. 177). There are also curious effects such as the wobbly pencil (p. 143), so it is highly surprising that the various parts of an object move together. This non-phenomenon does need ex-planation. The border-locking suggestion is that colour regions are normally locked to common luminance edges. Hence, the instability at isoluminance, where there are different colours but no brightness differences to give border-locking (p. xx).[9] In isoluminance, registration is lost.

DISTORTIONS OF TIME DELAY

Signals travel quite slowly along nerves, so the brain always receives sensory information after the event. Neural delay was first measured by Helmholtz in 1850. This was in the laboratory of his professor, Johannes Müller, who thought that nervous activity is so fast it would never be measured. (He even thought nerve signals travel faster than light, but this before Einstein.)

REACTION TIME

It is interesting to try Helmholtz's method for measuring reaction time, using say ten volunteers and a stopwatch. Place the volunteers in line, close together, and get the first to touch the second on the upper arm—who immediately touches his or her neighbour's upper arm—and so on along the line. Now repeat this; but touching near the wrist. This increases the total length of nerve, by the distance between shoulder and wrist multiplied by the number of subjects. Repeating the two conditions, say ten times, the average gives the delay quite accurately for the total length of nerve. The signals travel surprisingly slowly, about the speed of a bicycle.

When Helmholtz first measured neural delay, people were upset to discover that perceptions are out of date, and so we are not directly connected to reality.

It was found by astronomers, setting clocks from stars crossing a hairline in the eyepiece of a transit telescope, that delay is very different between highly trained observers. Each observer was characteristically different, so his 'personal equation' could be used to compensate his individual error. An observer's error can be *negative!* It can also be zero, evidently when the immediate future is correctly anticipated. Reaction time is far more complicated than physiological delay to a simple stimulus. A complication is that delay time is greater when there is more than one possible stimulus and more than one possible response—a point we have encountered before.

THE PULFRICH PENDULUM

There is a dramatic, simple phenomenon that makes it easy to measure increase in retinal delay in dim light. This is the *Pulfrich Pendulum*, which is well worth trying. A bob is suspended on a string, and set to swing across the line of sight. It is

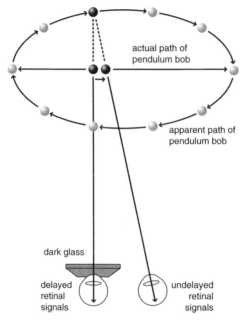

Figure 34. The Pulfrich Pendulum. Viewing a pendulum moving in a straight arc across the line of sight—with a dark glass over one eye—the bob seems to swing in depth, with an elliptical path. Its direction reverses, when the other eye views it through the dark glass. The reduced light gives the retinal delay mainly from dark adaptation. Both eyes signal the past, but the dimmer light pushes this eye further into the past. As the bob swings fastest at the middle of its swing, it is here the extra delay to one eye gives the greatest effective binocular disparity, and so the greatest depth.

viewed with both eyes, but with a dark glass (such as one filter of sunglasses) over one eye. Instead of appearing to swing in its straight arc, it appears to swing away and towards the observer in an elliptical path. The eccentricity of the ellipse can be measured by placing a pointer under its nearest and furthest apparent positions.

There is always a delay of signals from the eyes, but normally the same for each eye. The dark glass gives an extra delay to its eye, which has no effect when the bob is stationary, at the ends of its swing. But as the bob moves horizontally through its swing, the delayed signals are horizontally displaced for the delayed eye, which is the same as disparity giving stereo depth. The harmonic change of velocity generates an ellipse, and the delay can be calculated from the eccentricity of the illusory elliptical path.

The delay is mainly due to dark adaptation. So the effect occurs *in the reverse direction* when, instead of the dark filter, this eye is illuminated with a torch, giving light adaptation.

PULFRICH'S STRING

It is surprising that the effect is still seen with no marker under the bob, or any other obvious reference for stereo vision. How is this possible? The answer is—the string! If the string is made to keep vertical (with a very long string, or better with a parallelogram linkage), then the bob appears to move in its straight arc with no illusion.[10]

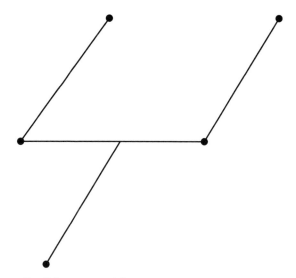

Figure 35. Parallelogram pendulum.

DELAYED VISION AND SPEECH

When sound or vision is delayed, especially by about half a second—speech, and drawing and writing, are upset. With time-delayed speech almost everyone stutters. With time-delayed vision (with electronically delayed television or on a computer screen) it is simply impossible to draw, or even to write one's own name while watching the delayed screen. This is important for remotely controlled skills, such as remote surgery by satellite link.

Although there is rapid adaptation to change of position—as with a displacing mirror, or a television camera at a position away from one's eyes—it seems one never adapts to, or compensates for time delay.

Cognitive Distortions

THE SIZE-WEIGHT ILLUSION

There are illusions that cut across different senses. These cross-model phenomena are important for showing that sensory systems are not separate, but generally work together. The size-weight illusion is an easily measured example of a clearly cognitive illusory phenomenon: smaller objects feel heavier than larger objects of the same scale weight. Why? A larger object is normally heavier than a smaller object, so perhaps larger objects, by setting up expectation of being heavier call up more muscle power to lift them—so they feel lighter. Related to this is the 'empty suitcase' effect. If one picks up an empty suitcase believed to be full, it may fly up into the air. These are cognitive phenomena depending on knowledge and assumptions—showing as illusions when knowledge or assumption is not appropriate to the situation.

Normally, discrimination is worse for heavy than for lighter objects—by Weber's Law. So, what happens to weight discrimination when a small object *feels* heavier, but is the *same* scale weight as a larger object? Does Weber's Law follow *scale* weight, or *apparent* weight? The answer is that discrimination is worse when the object is surprisingly light or surprisingly heavy.

Helen Ross found that discrimination is best (Fechner's constant[11] is smallest) for weights of a density of about 1, the density of water, and the body. That discrimination is worse with surprisingly heavy or surprisingly light objects, may have an explanation in engineering terms. It may suggest that that the nervous system is working like a Wheatstone bridge—comparing the external weight with an internal expectation. When the 'internal arm' of a bridge is set to nearly the value to be measured, the bridge is most sensitive and accurate.[12] This would go a long way to explaining the great dynamic range of the senses, together with their stability, though physiological components are labile. These are the great virtues of bridge circuits in electrical engineering.

We now turn to the classical visual distortion illusions. They intrigue children and have puzzled scientists for over a hundred years, and still do, as their significance remains controversial. Our expanded Peeriodic Table (pp. 242) is an attempt to give some order by classifying them by appearance and kinds of explanations. Distortions are the richest phenomena, as they receive the greatest variety of explanations. Crucial is whether they are due to disturbance of neural signals or whether the signals are misread. Both have examples, but to my mind the most interesting are due to misreading, as these suggest cognitive brain processes for seeing.

DISTORTIONS OF FLAT FIGURES RELATED TO DEPTH PERCEPTION

We live in a three-dimensional world, where distances and shapes of solid objects are vitally important, though the images in the eyes are flat.[13] A retinal image is essentially ambiguous, as it might be attributed to an infinite combination of sizes and distances and shapes of possible objects, though some are more likely than others. Distance is represented by many clues (or cues), but there is only one that is not inherently ambiguous—stereoscopic vergence of the eyes. But this is only reliable for quite near objects, as the base-line separation of the eyes is so small (about 65 mm). There is also stereo disparity: the differences of the retinal images as near and far objects have slightly different horizontal shifts, which though small are not ambiguous when the brain 'knows' which eye is which.[14] It is hardly surprising that distortions of size and shape are associated with the problem of perceiving distance, especially when stereo is not available; as for distant objects, and flat pictures representing depth. It is hardly surprising to find distortions in a picture representing depth though it is flat. We will come to this shortly.

For normal objects, their distances and three-dimensional shapes are far more important than the sizes and shapes of the retinal images. It is objects that we see. Although perception depends on the eyes' images these are not seen as objects are seen. They are *sources* but not *objects* of perception.

Although the formation of images from objects obeys simple rules of perspective projection, how the object is *seen* from the retinal image is complicated, and not fully understood. It is this that theories of perception attempt to describe and explain, and we still have a long way to go. A key is that perceptions are not slave to the eye's images. This is shown by the phenomenon we call constancy-scaling—that far from vision being slave to present images, we see objects as typical rather than their optically received sizes, shapes, and distances.

The images are neurally changed, by what we may call constancy-scaling.

Visual constancies of size and shape were appreciated by the seventeenth-century French philosopher René Descartes, who in his *Dioptrica* (1637) wrote:

> I need not, in conclusion, say anything special about the way we see the size and shape of objects; it is completely determined by the way we see the distance and position of their parts. Thus, their size is judged according to our knowledge or opinion as to their distance, in conjunction with the images that they impress upon the back of the eye. It is not the absolute size of the images that counts. Clearly they are a hundred times bigger [in area] when the objects are very close to us than when they are ten times further away; but they do not make us see the objects a hundred times bigger; on the contrary, they seem almost the same size, at any rate so long as we are not deceived by (too great) a distance.

This is a clear account of what we call size constancy. Descartes goes on to describe shape constancy:

> Again, our judgments of shape clearly come from our knowledge, or opinion, as to the position of the various parts of the objects and not in accordance with the pictures in the eye; for these pictures normally contain ovals and diamonds when they cause us to see circles and squares.

Many experiments have since been carried out on size and shape constancy, with measurements in various conditions.

Can constancy-scaling cause, as well as prevent, distortions? This idea is the basis of inappropriate scaling.

THE INAPPROPRIATE SCALING THEORY[15]

What sets size-scaling? Pictures, showing depth on a flat surface, are suggestive. They show that depth clues, such as perspective, can set scaling. This is so even when the picture is *seen* as flat; when depth represented by perspective convergence and other monocular depth clues is countermanded by texture of the picture plane, and so not seen. Texture preventing picture depth can be removed, as by painting in luminous paint and viewing in the dark with one eye; then the picture may appear in realistic depth. It is possible to measure the depth as seen, for visual space can be plotted by introducing a movable marker, seen stereoscopically and placed at selected positions in the apparent three dimensions of the picture. So visual space can be plotted in three dimensions, from flat pictures or illusion figures.[16]

Conversely, we can produce depth with no depth clues, as with a drawing of a wire cube, a Necker Cube. Though lacking depth clues—there is no perspective as the sides are parallel—it is seen as three dimensional, and it clearly flips in depth.

Even more interesting is a truly three-dimensional wire cube. This exhibits an astonishing range of evocative phenomena. When the wire cube flips in depth it *changes shape*. When *not* reversed, it looks like a true cube, though the image of the further face is smaller in the eye. But the cube has only parallel lines and lines at right angles.[17] There are no available depth clues. The seen sizes of the near and far faces simply follow their apparent distances.

As depth clues are not responsible for a wire cube appearing in three dimensions, with all its faces the same size (though the image of the further face is shrunk), we may suppose that Helmholtz's general principle is at work here—that *size is attributed according to seen distance* (as for Emmert's Law for the size of after-images seen at various distances, increasing in size with increased distance—see p. 196).

The key notion is that visual scaling can be set either 'upwards' by depth clues, or 'downwards' from seen depth.[18]

The wire cube is remarkably interesting when it flips in depth though its image in the eye is unchanged, for we can use it to separate upwards and downwards scaling. When depth-reversed, the cube becomes a *truncated pyramid*, with its further face too large, the distortion increasing as one approaches it. The apparent increase in size of the further face when the cube is depth-reversed is partly due to the trivial fact that the physically nearer (now apparently further) face gives a larger image, and partly from size-scaling following apparent distance, as in Emmert's Law and Helmholtz's principle.

These can be separated by viewing a *truncated wire cube* with the smaller face in front, from a distance giving the same-sized retinal images of the near and far faces.[19] Although the faces give the same retinal image, the apparently further one looks somewhat larger. So we see scaling following apparent distance. As it changes with apparent distance, with no change of the retinal image, this must be top-down scaling.

These phenomena tell us that size constancy can be set 'upwards' from depth clues or 'downwards' from the prevailing perceptual hypothesis of seen distance. When not appropriate to physical distance, either will produce corresponding distortions of size and shape though for different reasons.[20]

Also, a depth-reversed wire cube seems to move bizarrely as one moves around it—rotating to follow you, at twice your speed—as motion parallax is perceptually reversed when near and far are switched in perceptual depth. Whether the cube rotates *with* or *against* your movement is a sure sign for whether it is or is not depth-reversed.

Rules of bottom-up and top-down scaling
Bottom-up: Features *signalled* as further away are expanded.
Top-down: Features *appearing* as further away are expanded.

Any depth-cue may set size-scaling 'upwards'. Among the most powerful is perspective.[21] There are two especially powerful perspective shapes: *convergence* of parallel lines and the *arrow* shapes of corners. Converging lines and arrows are the key features of two of the best-known distortion illusions—the Ponzo and the Muller-Lyer.

For all these illusions, features represented as more *distant* are *expanded*. Normally this compensates the shrinking of retinal

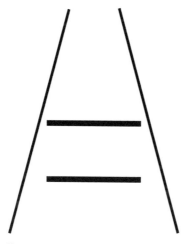

Figure 36. Ponzo illusion. The basic perspective illusion. The upper horizontal line appears expanded by constancy scaling, normally compensating shrinking of the retinol image with increased distance.

images with increased object distance; but for flat pictures this is inappropriate, as there is no optical shrinking with *represented* depth of a picture. Size-scaling for objects lying at different distances must be inappropriate for the surface of the picture, as it is flat. Indeed, scaling cannot be appropriate both for the picture and the surface on which it lies. The inappropriate constancy theory is that size-scaling produces distortions when set inappropriately to physical distance, as by perspective or other depth clues, so pictures are particularly subject to these distortions.[22]

Figure 37 shows some of the best-known perspective distortion illusions. They all follow the same rule: There is *expansion* with

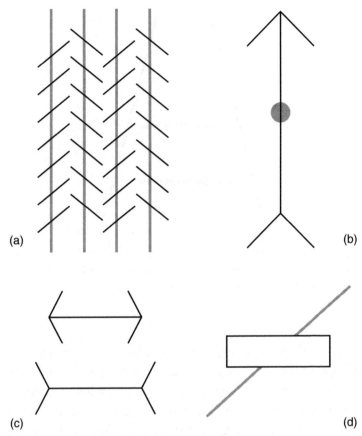

Figure 37. Well-known perspective distortion illusions: (a) Zöllner, (b) bisected Muller Lyer, (c) Muller-Lyer (d) Poggendorff.

distance depicted by perspective or other depth clues, though the figures are *flat*, and may be seen as flat.

It may be noted that these are all simple perspective drawings of familiar three-dimensional objects or scenes. Whenever greater *distance* is represented, *expansion* occurs.

The simplest is the converging lines of the (Figure 36) Ponzo figure, like a receding road or railway lines drawn in perspective. The Muller-Lyer (c) is a perspective drawing of a corner— (i) inside and (ii) outside—with illusory expansion again corresponding to depicted depth.

Right-angle corners are generally man-made, and the illusion occurs most strongly for people living in 'carpentered' environments, such as towns with squared buildings and parallel roads.

There are variations for the Muller-Lyer, such as semicircles instead of arrow corners—perspective drawings of cylinders— producing similar though weaker distortion illusions. There can also be depth signalled by other depth clues, such as occlusion.

The Zöllner (a) may be thought of as several walls at right angles.

In the Poggendorf (d), a (perspective) line passing behind a barrier appears displaced.

The distortions occur even when the perspective depth is not seen, or not noticed. This suggests that depth can be set quite directly by depth clues, and even when depth is countered by other clues, such as the texture of the surface of a drawing or illusion figure.

Are there any exceptions to the general principle that depicted *distance* gives *expansion*?[23] One has been suggested for the

Figure 38. Typical perspective scene: railway tracks.

Zöllner illusion. If the distorted lines are rotated by 90 degrees, to lie *along* instead of *across* the perspective convergence, the distortion reverses. The reason is not clear. Possibly this tells us something interesting about how scaling is set bottom-up by perspective.

DISTORTION FROM MISSING PERSPECTIVE

A rectangular table drawn *without* perspective appears to expand away from the observer. This is opposite to the normal shrinking of the image with increasing distance. Evidently, the drawing calls up knowledge of rectangular objects, and sets scaling 'top-down' to compensate the usual shrinking with distance. Here there is no shrinking, so we see the scaling as distortion. This can be a serious problem in engineering drawings.

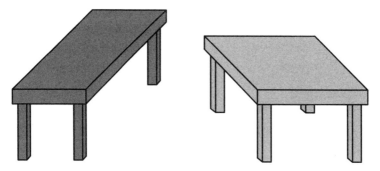

Figure 39. Distortion from assumed depth. Features that should from knowledge be further, and so optically shrunk at the eyes, are seen expanded by top-down scaling.

Early drawings and paintings of furniture look odd in this way, and this is a feature of Chinese pictures where the illusion is sometimes exaggerated by the artist.

THE HORIZONTAL-VERTICAL ILLUSION

This is simply a vertical line, rising from the centre of a horizontal line of the same length. The vertical appears considerably longer than the horizontal (Figure 40). (The effect is much less if the vertical is not at the centre of the horizontal.)

Does this have the same kind of size-scaling explanation as the Ponzo, the Muller-Lyer, and so on? If so, this is the minimum or simplest case and so has special interest. When the vertical line is in the middle of the horizontal it is compatible with

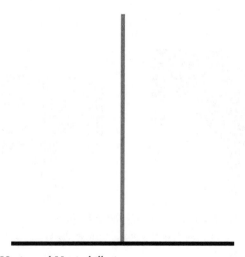

Figure 40. Horizontal-Vertical illusion.

converging perspective, though not when it is displaced from the centre.

The key to what may be happening can be seen by drawing this figure with luminous paint on black paper and viewing it glowing in the dark. The vertical line seems to tilt backwards. This is quite dramatic, especially when the line is quite long. In the world of objects, there are no very long vertical things—so a long vertical line in the retinal image is far more likely to be from something lying along the ground, such as a road going into the distance.

This illusion is rather unusual as the distortion depends on the orientation of the figure. Orientation also affects the Poggendorff illusion, which again is a minimal figure. Try rotating them slowly. The difference with orientation is striking.

Remarkably, a picture showing a vertical object such as a tall building, gives the horizontal-vertical distortion, even when the picture is placed horizontally on a table. It seems that picture *representation* of vertical can be adequate.[24]

ILLUSION DESTRUCTION BY APPROPRIATE SCALING

What would happen if the flat perspective figure was seen in correct 3D? The distortion is lost—destroyed—when the top-down and the bottom scaling are appropriate (Gregory and Harris 1975). This is strong evidence for the inappropriate constancy theory.

The Muller-Lyer is a particularly convenient figure to measure when presented as a corner in three dimensions, because the shafts of the arrow corners are at the same distance for both the inner and outer corners; so can easily be matched for measurement with an adjustable line at the same distance for both figures. This is best seen with wire model corners. They may be photographed in stereo and seen in 3D on a screen.[25]

The three-dimensional Ponzo, which may be made as a wire three-dimensional figure, also loses its distortion when seen in depth. But this is harder to measure, as it is difficult to compare sizes of features lying at different distances. Inspecting the other 'perspective' illusions in 3D depth gives the same result—the distortion is lost—though measurement is more difficult than for the Muller-Lyer, as the lines to be compared lie at different distances.[26]

The total absence of distortion seems to show that signal distortion has no significant role to play in these 'perspective' distortions. (This is a controversial claim and not all authorities on perception accept the inappropriate constancy theory.)

PERCEPTUAL 'PROJECTION'

'Projection' into surrounding space is essential to see external objects from images in the eyes. Similarly, sound vibrations in the ears seem to come from a distance, as belonging to external objects. Such psychological projection into the surrounding world does not apply nearly as much to the senses of taste and smell, called 'proximal' senses, which monitor temperature, and serve their owner with warnings of poison and promise safety of food.

Projection extends to tools. For the learner driver the car becomes an extension of the body, and a tennis player almost feels the end of the racket. Blind people experience the ground with the tip of the cane.

Staring in the dark at an object briefly illuminated by a flash of light (a photographic flash) produces a vivid after-image that may last for more than a minute. It is essentially a photograph on the retinas, but though physically in the eyes it is seen as out in space, lying on the surface of any object one is looking at. It may be near, as on the palm of one's hand, or 'projected' on a distant wall.

The projection of retinal after-images into external space, effectively demonstrates the general principle of 'reversed vision'. For normal vision is a two-way traffic, of light entering the eyes from external objects, and conversely the eye's images being psychologically projected out into external space and seen as objects. This psychological projection of image-to-object is immensely enriched by knowledge; that wood and metal are hard, water and milk wet, and so on for the great range of object properties we can recognize by vision.

As the brain confers object status to its eye's normal retinal images, seeing after-images as objects out there is essentially the same as for normal vision. There is, though, a time difference— as the after-image was formed a few seconds in the past, yet seen as though present in space and time. Out-of-date after-images cannot be distinguished from real-time perceptions, except that they move with the eyes. Of course all sensory inputs are strictly speaking out of date as there is always some neural delay from eye to brain.

Unlike normal retinal images of objects, after-images are fixed in size. They are like photographs, slowly fading, stuck on the retinas. They are remarkably useful, for teasing out and explaining processes of vision. The best known, and perhaps the most puzzling phenomenon of after-images, is known as Emmert's Law.

EMMERT'S LAW

An after-image 'projected' into external space appears *larger* when seen on a more *distant* surface or screen. More precisely, Emmert's Law states that an after-image increases in size linearly with the distance it appears to be.[27] This is exactly opposite to the *optical* shrinking of retinal images with increased object distance.[28]

Increase of apparent size with distance was noticed long before Emil Emmert announced his Law in 1881. It was noticed by Greek philosophers and scientists including Euclid. As the literature of perception abounds in confusing discussions of Emmert's Law, I just hope I shall not add to the confusions here!

The first question to ask is: does Emmert's Law apply to the *physical* distance of the surface on which it lies (as measured with a ruler), or to its *apparent* distance? These can be very different, as there are large illusions of distance.

The first alternative—physical distance—is surely impossible as distances are not given directly to the visual system, but are signalled indirectly with various depth clues, which are not entirely adequate or reliable. We should ask: what happens to Emmert's Law with an illusory distance? A robust error of distance is given by the odd-shaped Ames Room (see plate section). What happens if an after-image is seen on *apparently* equally distant, but *physically* different distant walls of an Ames Room? This has been tried.[29] We confirm that Emmert's Law follows *apparent* not *real* distance. This must indeed be so if perceived distance is given by clues to depth, rather than directly to physical distances, which is not how vision works.

HELMHOLTZ'S GENERAL PRINCIPLE FOR SEEING OBJECTS

The founder of modern understanding of perception—Hermann von Helmholtz (1821–94)—contributed immensely to understanding both the physiological and cognitive aspects of vision. He suggested a general principle for seeing objects from images:

> Objects are always perceived as being present in the field of vision as would have been there in order to produce the same

impression on the nervous system, the eyes being used under ordinary normal conditions.

Unfortunately this translation from the German is quite hard to understand or remember. Perhaps we may risk a simplification:

Objects are attributed *to images.*

I see a bowl of grapes on the table—as my brain *attributes* the images in my eyes to grapes, which I know from past experience, and they have a fair probability of being grapes.

Helmholtz recognized that errors of illusions may occur either when the nervous system is malfunctioning, or when functioning normally but in atypical conditions. He also saw that his principle could be run backwards—to infer from phenomena of illusions what the rules and assumptions for seeing are. As we might say, when perception takes off in illusion it shows its own colours and its battle plan as it is not anchored to the object world.

Helmholtz's principle is not limited to recognizing objects. It can apply to seeing size or motion, attributed to retinal signals as applying to what is out there. This may reveal what is going on for the old perceptual puzzles: Emmert's Law and the Moon Illusion.

What we attribute to retinal signals must be a central question for understanding seeing. A smile of pleasure may be attributed to pain in contexts where pleasure is unlikely, and the same smile becomes a grimace of pain in a torture chamber. Probabilities and context enter the scene as central players for attributions to images.

ATTRIBUTIONS OF SIZE AND DISTANCE

The changes of size of after-images in Emmert's Law are entirely different from the generally much smaller distortions of the Cafe Wall and the Ponzo and Muller-Lyer illusions. These distortions are usually less than 2:1, yet Emmert's Law size change may be many orders of magnitude, and seems to extend over the entire range of seen distances. It seems that scaling is set by bottom-up clues, while the Emmert's Law effect is top-down from the prevailing perceptual hypothesis of seen distance.

Comparing the sizes of objects at the same distance is a very different task from comparing sizes of objects at different distances. This is much more difficult, and the task is not simply defined. Does it mean the sizes the objects *would be* to the eye if they were at the same distance? We do not have conscious access to the size of the retinal image. It is a picture we can never see, and yet as the source of vision, it is the picture that gives us sight!

ZOOMING

Size-changing is familiar in photography with *zooming*. A zoom lens works by assigning more or less of the total field to the object of interest. When 'zoomed up' there is no increase in total information in the picture. The same is true of an optical microscope. Whatever the magnification, which may be as high as × 2,000, there is no increase in total information. We see this clearly with a digital camera, which has the same number of pixels available for a wide angle or telephoto lens. The long-focal-length telephoto lens gives a larger image of the subject of interest, at the cost of restricting the field of view. The total information set by the number of available pixels is the same for any zoom.

This is optical zooming, which is not available for unaided eyes. Digital cameras, however, also have internal electronic zooming. This steals pixels for a selected region from the rest of the picture. This looks like size-scaling.

THE HARVEST MOON ILLUSION

While high in the sky the Moon always looks about the same size, but when it is low on the horizon it may appear huge. This is the Harvest Moon illusion. There have been many theories, over the last two millennia, and suggested causes remain controversial.[30]

An explanation was offered in the second century BCE by the astronomer Ptolemy (Claudius Ptolemaeus).[31] In his book on optics, Ptolemy realized that the Moon illusion is not an optical phenomenon but is 'psychological'. He knew that the angle the Moon subtends to the eye is the same $(1/2^{\circ})$ when it is low on the horizon as when high in the sky. Ptolemy suggested as a psychological cause, that when near the horizon it appears to be *further* away, and so *larger*. This is invoking Emmert's Law. But there is a snag: people report seeing the Moon as appearing *nearer* when seen *larger*, near the horizon. This is opposite to Emmert's Law.

Ptolemy did not know that eyes have images. This was not appreciated before Kepler's understanding of the optics of the eye late in the sixteenth century. The Moon and the Sun subtend the same angle of 1/2°, though the Moon is 240,000 miles away and the Sun 93,000,000 miles distant. The Sun happens to be correspondingly larger (60 times larger and 60 times more distant), giving by an extraordinary chance the same-sized image of the Moon and the Sun to eyes on Earth.[32]

A small coin held at arm's length covers the Moon—so the Moon could be the size of a nearby coin or the far larger and more distant Sun—yet we see it about the size of an orange. Over the ocean on a clear night, it appears somewhat nearer than the horizon. One *sees* it at this sort of distance though one *knows* it is almost a quarter of a million miles away. As so often perceptual experience and explicit knowledge disagree.

It has been suggested that the inclination of the eyes is important for the Moon Illusion.[33] But the illusion is present, to much the same extent, when the Moon is seen not on the horizon but above a nearby mountain, though the eyes are inclined upward. Also, the illusion goes when the Moon is viewed through a tube, cutting out the surroundings. This can easily be confirmed by the reader. The phenomenon is related to the surrounding scene. The Moon appears larger when there are rich depth cues.[34] When low on the horizon, or above a mountain, there are surrounding texture and perspective depth cues that may scale up the size of the moon as in the Ponzo illusion. This increase in size makes it appear nearer, as the moon is not locked to a textured background.

The full answer for the Moon Illusion seems to be: (1) the Moon is scaled up in size by depth clues, as for the Ponzo and other such illusion distortion figures; (2) this increase in apparent size makes the Moon appear *nearer*; (3) when the corresponding illusion figures, especially the Ponzo, are presented on a textured paper surface they do not look nearer as they are locked to the surface; (4) but if the background is made invisible (as when the figure is drawn in luminous paint and viewed in darkness) then, like the Moon, the illusory expansion makes it *bigger* and *nearer*, so violating Emmert's Law. In short, Emmert's Law is violated when scaling modifies the size-distance trade-off of Helmholtz's principle.

VISUAL DEFAULTS?

This leaves another question: why does the Moon look the *same size* each time it is seen while high in the sky? In this instance, there are no obvious depth clues for scaling its size or distance. Tentatively we may introduce a new concept. In the absence of visual clues there may be *default* sizes and distances. (This notion is familiar in computing and word processors. In the absence of instructions they adopt default settings, which are typical, though may not be quite appropriate to the present situation.) A default assumption seems needed for the Moon to appear the same size, each time it is seen when high in the sky, without distance clues. This is a speculation but seems worth following up as a quite general principle for clueless perception.

THE MOVING MOON

There is another illusion of the Moon and stars: they seem to follow one as one moves. This is particularly clear when driving in an open car at night. It is as though strings attach the Moon and stars to the moving car. This is an *optical* illusion, with a quite simple answer.

The Moon and stars are so far away there is no significant change in the direction their light comes from as we move on Earth.[35] For nearby objects this can only happen for things moving with us. So we attribute movement to the Moon and stars, seeing them moving as we move. Perhaps for millennia this has been evidence that our comings and goings on Earth are linked to the heavens, so the gods take an interest in us. Hence astrology?

Notes

1. Consider dropping a book in the bath. It may be difficult to read because the print (the signals) is disturbed. Or very differently, you may misread clear print by selecting wrong meanings for the words.
2. One does not see one's own eyes moving in a mirror. Signals to the brain are cut off during saccadic (rapid) movements of the eyes.

3. People with eyes close together see greater depth with a stereoscope, because the compensation exaggerates stereo in 3D pictures.
4. See Gregory and Heard (1979, 1982, 1983).
5. This is also true of the Fraser Spiral.
6. Gregory and Heard (1982).
7. The rectangle is placed on the transparent front of a light box, and illuminated from the front, so can be made lighter or darker than the background. Either may be varied, to produce the 'phenomenal phenomenon' illusory motion.
8. The sudden switch of stereo depth across isoluminance is because fusion switches across the narrow edges—as fusion does not occur with opposite contrasts at the eyes. So, this is a special case.
9. In the Café Wall, the regions of contrasting brightness moving together across the neutral mortar lines might be due to 'border-locking', normally reducing signalling errors. For the neutral mortar lines would be the same to the visual system as signalled discrepancies of positions of edges. The idea is that contrasting regions get pulled together across narrow gaps, normally reducing errors of 'registration'. The design assumption is that it is better to have some distortion than extra contours, of failed registration. On this account, the illusory wedges do not occur when the mortar is darker or lighter than the tiles, as the border-locking would then be to the *near* sides of the mortar, not across it.
10. It is best to use a fairly short pendulum to give the effect with no other reference, as it is the change from vertical of the string that matters; but a long pendulum remains almost vertical as it swings, similarly to the parallelogram pendulum.
11. This is a constant in the equation in Weber-Fechner Law relating stimulus intensity to sensation. It may be thought of as background 'noise' in the nervous system.
12. This U-shaped function might be because weight discrimination works like a Wheatstone Bridge circuit; comparing the sensory (external) signal with the (internal) anticipated weight. Bridges have highest discrimination when these are nearly the same. Such

an arrangement would give the sensory system a large dynamic range and stability, in spite of its low dynamic range and labile biological components.

13. Of course the retina is curved, and so three-dimensional; but the image is flat in the sense that Holland is thought of as flat, though curved on the surface of the spherical Earth.

14. This is not available to consciousness, though is fairly well tagged in the stereo system.

15. R. L. Gregory (1963), 'Distortion of visual space as inappropriate constancy scaling', *Nature*, 199: 678–90.

16. This (subjective) depth can be measured objectively. The trick is to introduce a small moveable marker light into the picture optically, with a part-reflecting mirror (like Pepper's Ghost), and place the little light at the seen depth of selected regions of the picture. The picture is visible only to one eye, the marker light to both eyes; so avoiding stereoscopic information that the picture is flat, while allowing the marker to be positioned accurately in depth. (This is achieved with cross-polarization). This system allows the observer's private visual space to be plotted in three dimensions. It does, however, take some skill to use.

17. Nearer edges will hide small regions of further edges, which is the clue of *occlusion*, but the effect of this is to inhibit reversal. Visible occlusion can be avoided by painting the wire cube matt black; or even better, by coating it with luminous paint so it glows in the dark. One or other has been employed for these observations.

18. I first described this in Gregory (1963), page 678.

19. This can be done by varying the viewing distance until the near face occludes the further, or by finding the critical distance from their shadows cast by a point source of light.

20. The idea is that perspective convergence can set size-scaling quite directly 'bottom-up' (cf. Gregory 1963, 1998). So features represented as distant are expanded, which is so for these illusion figures. A test of this theory is to view them as three-dimensional models (inside and outside corners, for the Muller-Lyer 'arrows' illusion, or

in 3D stereoscopic depth). As the size-scaling set by these perspective shapes is now *appropriate* these distortions disappear, though the retinal images are essentially the same as for the usual flat figures (Gregory and Harris (1975)).

21. Perspective in pictures can even beat stereopsis. Try reversing the pictures in a stereoscope, so each eye sees the other's picture. The scene generally retains its perspective depth, against the reversed stereo.

22. This theory was first suggested in Gregory (1963). The key idea is that depth cues can set the scaling even though the figure *appears* flat. The other key idea is that scaling can be set in this way bottom-up—but can also be set top-down—as shown by the changes of ambiguous objects such as a wire cube, though the retinal image remains unchanged. Active ambiguity is very useful for identifying bottom-up and top-down scaling. The underlying physiology of scaling is now being investigated, especially at the California Institute of Technology.

23. This was discovered by Nicholus Humphrey and Michael Morgan (1965), when they were students at Cambridge. It could be evidence against the inappropriate scaling theory, or it could be telling us something about how scaling works. The jury is out.

24. It seems that the Horizontal-Vertical illusion is greater when the figure or the object is large. This seems to be so, even when it *appears* larger but has the same-sized retinal image. By using the trick of projecting on to screens of different distances (when of course the distant picture is larger) and placing the eyes at the position of the projector's lens—we see a larger distant and smaller nearer picture with the *same size* images in the eyes. Under these conditions the H-V illusion is larger, though the eye's images are exactly the same. This is a further indication that it involves (Bayesian) cognitive brain processing.

25. Shown as anaglyphs in Gregory, *Eye and Brain* (4th edition).

26. Evidently it is not the slight differences of retinal images for stereo that matters—but rather *seeing depth appropriately* by any means.

When depth is seen correctly with a single eye (a bit of motion parallax, with one eye, can help) the distortion goes when the depth is seen. This is clearly a top-down effect.

27. E. Emmert (1881), 'Grössenverhältnisse der Nachilder', *Klinische Monatsblätter fur Augenheilkunde* 19: 443–50.

28. R. L. Gregory, J. G. Wallace, and F. Campbell (1959), 'Changes in the size and shape of visual after-images seen in complete darkness during changes of position space', *Quarterly Journal of Experimental Psychology* 11: 54-5.

29. J. Dwyer, R. Ashton, and J. Boerse (1990), 'Emmert's Law in the Ames Room', *Perception* 19, 35–41; J. Boerse, R. Ashton, and C. Shaw (1992), 'The apparent shape of after-images in an Ames Room', *Perception* 21: 262–8.

30. The history of the Harvest Moon illusion is discussed very fully by Helen Ross and Cornelis Plug, *The Mystery of the Moon Illusion*, (Oxford: Oxford University Press, 2002).

31. Claudius Ptolemeus, a mathematician, geographer, astronomer, astrologer, was born after CE 85 and died c. CE 168 in Roman-occupied Egypt.

32. Their subtended angle being the same is of course why we have solar eclipses, when the Sun's corona becomes dramatically visible against a black sky in daytime. There is an apparent expansion of the Sun, as for the Moon, when low on the horizon, though it is dangerous to look at the sun.

33. A. F. Holway and E. G. Boring (1941), 'Determinants of apparent visual size with distance variant', *American Journal of Psychology* 54: 21–37.

34. This is the basis of the well-known account given by Lloyd Kaufman and the late Irvin Rock (L. Kaufman and I. Rock (1962), 'The Moon Illusion', *Scientific American* 136: 1023-31. But this account makes the wrong prediction, saying the moon looks *further* on the horizon, though it is reported as looking *nearer*. My view is, it is scaled bottom-up by perspective and texture gradients to make it look

larger, and so it looks nearer. This is contrary to Emmert's Law. (Lloyd Kaufman told me recently that he accepts this interpretation.)

35. For high-speed flying, this is somewhat different, as the Earth is curved. Also there is lack of reference as generally Earth objects are not seen at the same time as the stars, as when for example we are moving and looking up through trees.

FICTION

Fictions are not necessarily false. Indeed, wholly false fictions would hardly have meaning, or be visible. We assume that a fictional character in a novel has the usual single head and two eyes, eats breakfast, and finds illusions of some interest. It is very hard to communicate, or understand or see, complete fictions.

Seeing familiar objects in inkblots shows how we people and furnish fictions with accepted facts. Even the most bizarre aliens in science fiction are rearrangements of life on earth. Vision furnishes the external world with objects attributed to retinal images. We see this happening in the case of *after-images*, which we have met before. Artists rely on this process in the viewer to give meaning to marks on the canvas. These are more facts from the viewer's past than the artist's present fiction.

After-images

In a lightning storm on a dark night, after-images can be so vivid they are hard to separate from object reality. This is hardly surprising, as after-images are essentially the same as normal retinal images, though continuing for an abnormal time. They are for a few seconds photographs fixed in the eyes, moving like photographs from fact to fiction as reality changes through time.

Contours

Contours and edges are signalled with specialized neural systems, recorded by physiologists with microelectrodes from single cells, discovered by the American physiologists David Hubel and Torstin Weisel (1962). They found cells in the visual cortex responding to particular orientations of lines and other cells responding to movement, some to movement in only one direction. This turned out to be a physiological alphabet of responses to kinds of stimuli. What happens further along deeper in the brain is not so clear, though cells are found responding to more general features—'complex' and 'hyper-complex' cells. This research gives basic understanding of how the visual brain is organized.

Illusory contours

Contours and surfaces can be seen in blank regions where there are no stimulus differences. An example is Figure 41.

These three cakes, each with a slice cut out, are seen to have a ghostly illusory triangle joining the missing slices. The Italian artist and psychologist Gaetano Kanizsa created this and several other such dramatic figures. Illusory contours are to be found in illuminated manuscripts a millennium old, and even in cave paintings, but were ignored by visual scientists until Kanizsa's dramatic examples appeared in *Scientific American* in 1950 (Kanizsa 1950). Yet, almost as striking were figures produced fifty years earlier by a German psychologist Fredarich Schumann (Schumann 1900). Oddly, their significance was not recognized for half a century, even though Schumann's

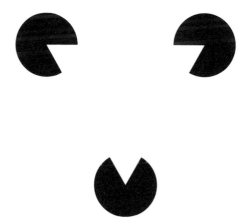

Figure 41. Kanizsa triangle.

example was seen by thousands of students in textbooks such as *Principles of Psychology* by R. H. Woodworth (1938) and earlier. They were hardly discussed in the textbooks or noticed by the students. Presumably illusory contours did not fit the prevailing paradigm of perception as stimulus-driven, and so were almost entirely ignored. This was so before Kanizsa's beautiful examples, which were too striking to be ignored, and paradigms for perception were starting to change—being extended to include active top-down processing. By the early 1970s, I for one, was sure that these illusory contours and ghostly surfaces were probability-induced fictions created by the visual system and working top-down into visual experience (Gregory 1972):

> The cognitive paradigm of perception regards perceptions as hypotheses, selected by sensory data, but going beyond available data, to give 'object hypotheses' (Gregory 1970). This paradigm would be satisfied by supposing that the illusory object is 'postulated' as a perceptual hypothesis to account for the blank sectors and the breaks in the triangle.

Every day we recognize objects although parts are hidden by nearer things. Our brains create much of what we see by adding what 'ought' to be there. We only realize that the brain is guessing when it guesses wrongly, to create a clear fiction.

The fictional triangle must be seen as lying in front of the cakes. If it is forced back to behind the cakes (by using stereopsis), it disappears (Gregory and Harris 1974). The point is, it is very unlikely that cut-outs of cakes would line up exactly—much more likely that there is some triangle-shaped object in front hiding these regions. If we rotate the cakes slightly, the illusory edges become curved. Then, with a greater rotation, they snap and disappear.

Bottom-up or top-down?

Whether illusory contours are signalled bottom-up from surrounding features, or inferred from unlikely gaps, is a crucial decision for classifying them and seeing what they mean as phenomena of vision. That they can be *curved interpolations*, between contours or edges that are misaligned, is against a bottom-up account and strongly favours a top-down explanation that illusory contours are cognitive creations, here based on slightly misaligned cuts of the cakes.

Illusory contours have effects essentially the same as normal contours. For example they produce the same distortions and many other illusions. They seem indeed to be very similar to normal contours—suggesting that normal 'true' contours have a strong cognitive component. This idea is captured by the archaeological drawings which show alternative constructions (or rather reconstructions) of early huts from the evidence of post holes—including various possible rabbit holes (see Figure 42). Prior beliefs (huts built at that time were circular, or might be rectangular) changed the significance of the available data. Visual research in the 1970s suggested that contours are similarly constructs based on probabilities. It is suggestive that lines on a graph of data-points need not touch any of the data-points, yet are accepted as what they represent. For

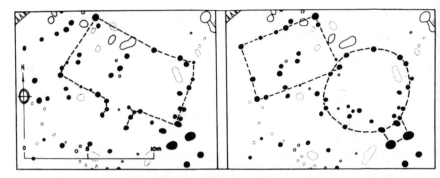

Figure 42. The black dots are holes found in an actual archaeological dig. One group of archaeologists selects a set of the holes as post holes—data— and rejects others as irrelevant. Other archaeologists select some different holes as data and form different hypothetical huts.

empirical science, the data-points are thrown away while the fictional plotted curve is retained as the accepted truth. The same seems to hold for vision: we do not see the images in our eyes, but rather cognitive constructs based on all manner of data and edited by what is probably true from past experience.

The Hermann Grid

The German visual scientist Günter Baumgartner suggested an explanation for these light or dark splodges at the intersection of a grid, to what is called the *centre surround* organization of retinal ganglion cells. Some have 'on' centres and 'off' surrounds; in other cells this is reversed. The idea is that in the intersections of a light grid the surrounds are stimulated more than the centres. The smudges are not seen in the fovea where the eyes are aiming, because foveal ganglion cells have very small receptive fields, so both surrounds and centres are stimulated at the intersections. As pointed out recently by Peter Schiller and Christina Carvey (2005), the smudges disappear when the grid lines are not straight. So line detectors seem to be important, but this is not understood.

Seeing your blind spot

We have seen that the eye is rather like a digital camera, with over 100 million light-sensitive 'rod' and 'cone' receptor cells on the retina. Signals from these receptors go to the brain along the one million fibres of the optic nerve. The spot where these come out of the retina is totally blind, as there are no receptors. Yet we seldom see blackness, or nothing, in this surprisingly large blind region. Why don't we see the blind region as a black hole in visual space? The American philosopher Daniel Dennett has suggested that it is *ignored*, like a boring person at a party who does not contribute. This is an important idea, though the evidence now favours the alternative, that there is active filling-in from the surrounding colour and pattern. But the brain cannot fill in for an isolated object that (as we can easily demonstrate) disappears when its image falls on the blind region in the eye.

O   *

Try closing your right eye and look at the star with your left eye. Move your head slowly nearer or further—the circle should disappear at a certain distance. It disappears when its image in the eye falls on the blind region. But note: the surrounding colour and brightness are seen in the blind region, though no signals are reaching the brain. If you look at any scene (such as a page of this book), you will not be aware of the blind region and it will not be black. Your brain creates what 'ought' to be there in the blind region.

Normally the other eye is open, so can provide the missing information. But here only one eye is open and yet the blind region is not 'seen'. There is evidence that the blind region of each eye is filled in by active processes at the first stage of visual processing in the brain (in area V_I). The neurologist V. S. Ramachandran and I created an artificial blind region (a scotoma) by staring fixedly at a small pattern on a computer screen, or a region of visual noise (looking like a small swarm of ants). We found that when the observers then looked at a blank screen of nearly the same brightness and colour, much the same now invisible coloured patch, or region of noise, would appear—evidently created in the brain and 'projected' into visual space. This active cortical creation is confirmed with recent experiments using fMRI (Functional Magnetic Imaging.) The filling-in of scotomas and the blind spot is a remarkable process that saves us from seeing threatening forms hovering around the centre of vision. Much of seeing is fictional.

PARADOX

Unlikely and impossible

A statement or a perception may be too *unlikely* to be possible, or may be *logically* impossible. Swimming the Atlantic is too *unlikely*. A dark blonde is *logically* impossible. The first—empirical impossibility—is judged to be too unlikely from knowledge of the world. The second—logical paradox—is inconsistent with symbolic rules, especially how words are used. Our language does not permit saying, 'She is a dark-haired blonde'. Language does, however, allow, 'He swam the Atlantic', though we would not believe it. A few years ago we would not believe 'He walked on the Moon'. This was just too unlikely, though it has happened.

It is generally true that unlikely things are harder to see than probable things. And we tend to see things we expect. Such effects are, however, quite hard to demonstrate as consistent phenomena. One way is to use flipping ambiguous figures, where one alternative is more likely than others. Examples of flipping ambiguity, such as the Duck-Rabbit (Figure 16), are drawn to balance the probabilities of the alternatives. It is interesting to take this or other examples and modify them. If the ears are enhanced, it will more often be seen as a rabbit. The Vase-Faces drawing is easy to modify to make the faces or the vase more or less probable. The Necker Cube (Figure 17) is about equally seen in each orientation; but if it is drawn with perspective, it will be more stable when the smaller face is seen as more distant, being seen more often and for longer periods.

With very limited information, only likely objects can be shown consistently. This is shown elegantly in Johansson's experiments, in which human figures in motion are seen from a few little lights placed at the joints—the elbows, knees and so on.—This does not work for less familiar objects, such as a toy machine, when many more little lights are needed to see it.

Empirically impossible

When a lot of information is provided we can see empirically impossible objects, though they look puzzling. A good example is René Magritte's horse in a wood. (Plate 3). We see a horse though we know it could not be ridden, as it could not be alive, yet we see the impossible horse.

One might well ask why we can see highly unlikely objects, though generally more likely objects are favoured and more easily seen. Doubtless the reason is that unlikely things and events do occur, and may need special attention to deal with them. Perceptual learning would be impossible if we were blind to the unlikely. But why can we see logical impossibilities that will never occur?

Perceptual paradoxes

The general answer, I think, for why we have visual paradoxes is that perceptions are hypotheses and hypotheses depend on *rules*, which may conflict, and on *assumptions* that may be wrong. There can also be conflicting *data*, especially when one or more of parallel channels provide incorrect information.

Sensory signal paradoxes

As the senses work with many parallel channels, there are plenty of opportunities for conflicting signals to create paradoxes. This kind of situation is familiar in science, such as when instruments disagree with each other, and in normal life when witnesses of an accident give different accounts of it. A judge who was offered: 'She was in a blue car travelling east', and also: 'He was on a red motor-bike going north' must dismiss one account, or assume these were different people, to avoid a paradox. Automatic landing systems have several separate computers; if one differs markedly from the others it is rejected. Rejection is useful for avoiding paradox. No doubt the brain rejects a great deal of conflicting information. This may be conflicting signals, or conflicts with knowledge.

Hot and cold

We have mentioned Berkeley's paradox of tepid water feeling hot and cold at the same time, when one hand is adapted to cold water and the other to hot (p. 80). Although it is impossible for an object (including water) it is entirely possible for one hand to *feel* it as cold and the other hand as hot. Similarly, two thermometers might indicate that water is 90° and 100°, if they are not calibrated.

There can be paradoxical hot-cold sensation from the same hand. The skin has small regions of nerve endings signalling hot, others cold. Over-stimulating a 'cold' spot can give a sensation of heat; so heat can produce hot and cold sensations at the same time. This can also be produced by feeling closely spaced hot and cold pipes. The mixed hot-cold sensation is peculiar. It doesn't seem impossible, just peculiar and hard to describe.

Movement is seen, impossibly, without change of position in the after-effect of motion. This is another *signal* paradox due to parallel channels for position and motion, signalling differently. It is like conflicting witnesses.

The Shepard Tone

There is at least one powerful 'signal' hearing paradox—Roger Shepard's Impossible Tone. It continues to rise (or fall) in pitch forever, without getting anywhere. It has rich changing harmonics that feed through, upwards or downwards, giving the sensation of a continually changing note though on average it does not change. This is rather similar to visual movement without change of positions in the after-effect of a rotating spiral.[1]

Cognitive paradoxes

An early paradoxical figure was a beautiful design by Oscar Reutersvärd for Swedish stamps (1932) (Figure 43).

Figure 43. Impossible Swedish stamps.

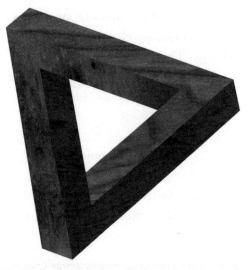

Figure 44. Impossible triangle.

Best for seeing what is going on is the Impossible Triangle of the distinguished scientists (father and son) Lionel and Roger Penrose (1958). (I think I was the first to show that this can be made as a three-dimensional object, from three straight lengths of wood, appearing impossible from certain positions.)[2] This shows what is happening (Figure 44). The lengths of wood appear to touch at all three corners, though at one corner they don't. They seem to be the same distance, though they are not, because of a visual rule: *things touching are the same distance.* Normally this rule works well, but it is entirely possible for things to touch optically, in the retinal image, and yet not touch physically in the external world, as they may be at different distances and line up to the eye. The triangle looks impossible because vision assumes that the three pieces of wood are at the same distance, as they appear to touch at the corners. This assumption is false.

Although we know intellectually that it is false, the visual system continues with its false assumption—to generate the paradox. (The principle is also seen in Hogarth's engraving of 1754, *The Fisherman* (Figure 22)).

The strange fact that the triangle continues to *appear* impossible even when we *know* the answer shows the modularity of the brain. The modularity here is that *perceptions* are generated separately from *conceptions*. This is a beautifully clear example of one part of the brain knowing the answer intellectually and yet being unable to help the visual brain.

Illusions in animals

It is not easy to measure illusions in animals, so there are rather few reliable studies, especially in primates. But there are a number of interesting experiments on insects and birds. Especially intriguing is the work of Irene Pepperberg at MIT with talking parrots. A very well trained parrot can identify which is a larger or smaller object by reporting in English, and also the colour of an object. So Irene Pepperberg can use the parrot's speech almost as though it is a human observer. With her colleagues, she finds that not only does the parrot show the usual size illusion, but the distortion is affected by various conditions similarly as for a human observer. She attributes the illusion to the bird's experience of 'carpentered' environments (Segall, Campbell, and Herskovitz 1966), but aims to test birds living in different conditions.

Notes

1. I played the Shepard Tone on the radio programme 'Desert Island Discs', and received furious letters from musicians!
2. R. L. Gregory, *The Intelligent Eye* (London: Weidenfeld, 1970).

CHAPTER 6

EPILOGUE: FROM PERCEPTIONS TO CONSCIOUSNESS

The most mysterious output of the brain is consciousness. Some, though not all, perceptions are associated with *qualia*—sensations of red, bright, black and so on. How qualia are generated by the brain is deeply mysterious. But perhaps we should not be worried that qualia of sensation and the physiological processes generating them are so different. It is not unusual for combinations of causes to be very different from the result. For example, oxygen and hydrogen combine to produce water, which has very different properties. Assembling a model from a construction kit makes, say, a working model clock with quite different properties from the bits of metal in the box. And the mechanism of a clock is extremely different from the (mysterious) time it records.

Flagging the present

What, if anything, do qualia do? From how we think about perception—as richly cognitive, with knowledge from the past to interpret the present and far removed from present stimuli—we might hazard a guess on what qualia do. Given evolution and natural selection, we should expect consciousness to have some survival-enhancing function. Perception is based on ancient, innate, and on more recent learned knowledge from the past, with present information from the senses for real-time behaviour. As perception depends on knowledge from the past, there must be a problem distinguishing present events from memories, and also from anticipations of the future (Gregory 1998). Is it possible that qualia of consciousness serve to *flag the present moment?*

The present is signalled by real-time stimuli from the senses; but as perceptions are largely stored knowledge, the present moment needs to be identified for behaviour to be appropriate to what is happening here and now. When crossing a road one needs to know that the traffic light seen as red is red *now*, and not a remembered past or an anticipated future red light. For behaviour to be useful, it must be in real time. Qualia of the present have a special vividness that is seldom or never experienced in memory.

A self-experiment

Try looking at some distinctive coloured object, such as a red tie. Then close the eyes, and imagine the tie. The vivid qualia of vision suddenly dims in the imagination of memory. Isn't it this vividness that makes the perceived present 'real' and now?

Try the experiment in reverse. With the eyes shut, imagine an object such as the red tie—then open the eyes and look at it. The qualia of the present are startlingly vivid by comparison with the memory. Perhaps qualia prevent us from confusing the present with remembered past or anticipated future.

Some exceptions that 'prove the rule'

There are suggestive exceptions to recognizing the present. A famous example is the case of Mr S, described by the Russian neuropsychologist Alexander Luria (Luria 1969). Mr S was a professional memory man. His vast memory and extremely vivid imagination became confused with real-time reality to the point of danger, as when he confused present with remembered traffic lights. He said, 'I'd look at a clock and for a long while continue to see the hands fixed just as they were, and not realise time had passed ... that's why I'm often late.'

Vivid qualia unrelated to present sensory signals are experienced in dreams. In sleep the present moment has no special significance, for behaviour is absent or minimal and not related to present events. When sensory inputs are cut off or ignored, perception may become abnormal. This occurs in isolation situations, when sensory stimulation is absent over many hours. In hallucinogenic drug-induced states and in schizophrenia, vivid qualia are experienced with no sensory input; though similar brain activity seems to be present (Kosslyn *et al.* 1995).

It is reported that in drug-induced states time may seem to stop. In *The Doors of Perception* Aldous Huxley describes changes of consciousness experienced with mescaline. He ceases to be interested in action, becoming a passive observer ('the will suffers a profound change for the worse'), though his ability to think straight is little if at all reduced. So he becomes almost 'a Not-self'. Most suggestive, 'Visual impressions are greatly intensified', while 'interest in space is diminished and interest in time falls almost to zero'. Huxley emphasizes that colours are immeasurably enhanced in vividness, ordinary objects appearing self-luminous, with the inner fire of jewels, while time essentially stops, becoming 'an indefinite duration or alternatively a perpetual present'. With mescaline and other hallucinogenic drugs sensations become enhanced—super-qualia—and the present is emphasized with correspondingly little flow of time.

The notion that qualia normally flag the present does not begin to explain how qualia are produced by brain processes. Much remains mysterious. But it has implications for consciousness in other animals. As perception evolved to become more intelligent through evolution, it drew away from direct control by stimuli, as it depended increasingly on hypotheses of what might be out there. So identifying what is out there *now* must have become an increasing problem with development of cognitive brain function.

Intelligence cannot be tied to the sensed present for intelligence solves anticipated problems. Intelligence frees us from the tyranny of moment-to-moment control by the senses, but at the cost of uncertain here and now. It is a speculation that qualia are useful for flagging the present, but as the tortoise said, 'I can't take a step forward without sticking my neck out.'

REFERENCES

1 Paradigms of Perception

Bird, Alexander (2001), *Thomas Kuhn*. Princeton University Press.

Cottingham, J., Stoothoff, R., and Murdock, D. (eds) (1985), *The Philosophical Writings of Descartes*. Cambridge: Cambridge University Press.

Dawkins, Richard (1976), *The Selfish Gene*. Oxford: Oxford University Press.

Gregory, R. L. (1974), Paradigms of Perception. *Proceedings of the Royal Institution, London*: 117–39.

—— (1981), *Mind in Science*. London: Weidenfeld & Nicolson.

—— (1997), Knowledge in perception and illusion. *Philosophical Transactions of the Royal Society of London B*, 352: 1121–8.

Hubel, D. H. and Weisel, T. N. (1962), Receptive fields, binocular interaction and functional architecture in the cat's visual cortex. *Journal of Physiology* 160: 106–64, and others.

Hyman, A. (1982), *Charles Babbage*. Oxford: Oxford University Press.

Korb, K. B. and Nicholson, A. E. (2004), *Bayesian Artificial Intelligence*. London: Chapman & Hall.

Kune, Thomas (1962), *The Structure of Scientific Revolutions*. Chicago: University of Chicago Press.

Luria, Alexander (1969), *The Mind of a Mnemonist: A Little Book about a Vast Memory*. New York: Cape.

Nagel, T. (1974), What is it like to be a bat? *Philosophical Review* 83: 435–50.

2 Neuro-Archaeology

Adamson-Macedo, Elvedina N. (2002), *The Psychology of Pre-term Neonates*. Heidelberg: Mates Verlog.

Aglioti, S., de Souza, J. F., Goodale, M. A. (1995), Size contrast illusions deceive the eye but not the hand. *Current Biology* 5: 679–85.

Bowler, Peter J. (1989), *Evolution: The History of an Idea*. Berkeley: University of California Press.

Buss, David M. (1999), *Evolutionary Psychology*. Boston: Allyn & Bacon.

Chomsky, N. (1957), *Syntactic Structures*. The Hague: Mouton.

—— (1980), *Rules and Representations*. New York: Columbia University Press.

Coghill, G. E. (1914–36), Correlated anatomical and physiological studies of the growth of the nervous system of Amphibia. *Journal of Comparative Neurology*, Parts I to XII.

Critchley, Macdonald and Critchley, Eileen (1998), *John Hughlings Jackson: Father of English Neurology*. Oxford: Oxford University Press.

Darwin, Charles (1873), *The Expression of the Emotions in Man and Animals*. London: John Murray. Reprinted University of Chicago Press (1965). For current views: Paul Ekman (1973), *Darwin and Facial Expression: A Century of Research in Review*. New York: Academic Press.

Gesell, Arnold (1945), *The Embryology of Behaviour: The Beginnings of the Human Mind*. New York: Harper.

Goddard, S. (1995), *A Teacher's Window into the Child's Mind: A Non-Invasive Approach to Learning and Behaviour Problems*. Eugene, OR Fern Hill Press.

—— (2002), *Reflexes, Learning and Behaviour: A Window into the Child's Mind*. Chester: INPP.

Goodale, M. A. and Milner, A. D. (1992), Separate Visual Pathways for Perception and Action. *Trends: Neuroscience* 15: 20–5.

Gould, Stephen J. (1980), *The Panda's Thumb: More Reflections in Natural History*. Harmondsworth: Penguin.

Gregory, R. L. (1970), *The Intelligent Eye*. London: Weidenfeld & Nicolson.

Grzegorz, Królickzak, Heard, P., Goodale, M. A., and Gregory, R. L. (2006), Dissociation of perception and action unmasked by the Hollow-Face illusion. *Brain Research* 1080, Elsevier B.V.: 9–16.

Hill, H. and Bruce, V. (1993), Independent effects of lighting, orientation and stereopsis on the Hollow-Face illusion. *Perception* 22: 887–97.

Huffman, D. A. (1968), Decision criteria for a class of 'impossible' objects. *Proceedings of the first Hawaii International Conference on System Sciences, Honolulu.*

—— (1971), *Impossible Objects as Nonsense Sentences*. Machine Intelligence no. 6, ed. Bernard Meltzer and Donald Michie. Edinburgh: Edinburgh University Press.

Kennedy, James G. (1978), *Herbert Spencer*. Boston: G. K. Hall.

Magnus, R. (1925), Animal Posture (Croonian Lecture). *Proceedings of the Royal Society*, B 98: 339–53.

Milner, A. D. and Goodale, M. A. (1995), *The Visual Brain in Action*. Oxford: Oxford University Press.

Pinker, Steven (1994), *The Language Instinct*. London: Allen Lane, The Penguin Press.

Ridley, Matt (1993), *The Red Queen*. Harmondsworth: Penguin Books.

Taylor, Michael W. (2007), *The Philosophy of Herbert Spencer*. London: Continuum.

Tooby, John and Cosmides, Leda (1992), Psychological Foundations of Culture, in J. Barcow, Leda Cosmides, and John Tooby (eds), *The Adapted Mind*. Oxford: Oxford University Press.

Wilson, E. O. (1975), *Sociobiology: A New Synthesis*. Cambridge, MA: Harvard University Press.

Wolpert, Lewis (1998), *Principles of Development*. Oxford: Oxford University Press.

3 First Light

Anstis, S. (1974), A chart demonstrating variations in acuity with retina position. *Vision Research* 14: 589–92.

Bakewell, Frederick Collier (1853), *A manual of electricity, practical and theoretical*, 2nd edn (1857) London.

Darwin, C. (1844), *Essay*.

—— (1849), *The Origin of Species*.

Darwin, Erasmus, (1803), *The Temple of Nature*.

Dawkins, R. (1976), *The Selfish Gene*. Oxford: Oxford University Press.

—— (1986), *The Blind Watchmaker*. New York: Norton.

Della Porta, Giovanni Battista (1589), *Natural Magic*.

Dennett, Daniel C. (1995), *Dangerous Idea*. London: Allen Lane, Penguin Press.

Descartes, R. (1664), *Treatise of Man*, English trans. 1972 by T. S. Hall. Cambridge, MA: Harvard University Press.

Grant, Edward (2007), *A History of Natural Philosophy*. Cambridge: Cambridge University Press.

Gregory, R. L. (1964), A technique for minimizing the effects of atmospheric disturbance on photographic telescopes. *Nature* 2003: 274–5.

—— (1966), *Eye and Brain*, 1st edn. London: Weidenfeld & Nicholson. 5th edn (1997) Oxford: Oxford University Press.

—— and Gombrich E. H. (eds) (1973), *Illusion in Nature and Art*. London: Duckworth.

Gruber, Howard E. (1974), *Darwin on Man: Early and Unpublished Notebooks*, annotated by Paul H. Barrett. New York: Dutton.

Hardie, Roger C. (1989), Sigmund Exner: *The Physiology of the Compound Eyes of Insects and Crustaceans*. Berlin: Springer-Verlag, 93–7. Translated from the (unattainable) German original: *Die Physiologie der facettierten Augen von Krebsen und Insecten* (1891).

Hoffstadter, D. R. and Dennett, Daniel C. (1945), *The Mind's Eye*. New York: Basic Books.

Land, M. F. and Nilsson, D.-E. (2002), *Animal Eyes*. Oxford: Oxford University Press.

Lyell, Charles (1830), *Principles of Geology*. 1997 edn. London: Penguin.

Nagel, T. (1974), What is it like to be a bat? *Philosophical Review* 83: 435–50.

Sarnat, H. B. and Netsky, M. G. (1974), *Evolution of the Nervous System*. 1981 edn. New York: Oxford University Press.

Wilkie, J. S. (1953), *The Science of Mind and Brain*. London: Hutchinson's University Library.

4 Unlocking Locke

Berkeley, G. (1709), *Essay on a New Theory of Vision*.

Dennett, Daniel. C. (1991), *Consciousness Explained*. London: Penguin.

Locke, J. (1690), *Essay Concerning Human Understanding*.

Newton, I. (1704), *Opticks*.

Russell, Bertrand (1945), *A History of Western Philosophy*. New York: Simon & Schuster.

5 Kinds and Causes

Adrian, Lord A. D. (1928), *The Basis of Sensation* and (1932) *Mechanisms of Nervous Action*. Cambridge: Cambridge University Press.

Craik, Kenneth (1943), *The Nature of Explanation*. Cambridge: Cambridge University Press.

Gibson, J. J. (1950), *Perception of the Visual World*. Boston: Houghton Mifflin.

Hick, W. E. (1952), The rate of gain of information. *The Quarterly Journal of Experimental Psychology* 4.1: 11–26.

Hubel, David (1988), *Eye, Brian and Vision*. New York: Scientific American Library of Science.

Kanizsa, Gaetano (1955), Margini: quasi-percettivi in campi con stimolazione omogenea. *Revista di psicologia* 49.1: 7–30.

—— (1976), Subjective contours. *Scientific American* 234: 48–52.

Melchner, I., Pallas, S. I., and Sur, M. (2000), Visual behaviour mediated by retinal projections directed to the auditory pathway. *Nature* 404.6780 (20 April): 871–6.

Miller, G. A. (1956), The Magic Number 7 plus or minus 2: Some Limits on our Capacity to Process Information. *Psycological Review* 63: 81–97.

Penrose, L. S. and Penrose, R. (1956), Impossible objects: a special type of illusion. *British Journal of Psychology* 49: 31.

Popper, Sir Carl (1972), *Objective Knowledge.* Oxford: Clarendon Press.

Shannon, Claude and Weaver, W. (1949), *The Mathematical Theory of Information.* Urbana, IL: University of Illinois Press.

Ungerleider, L. G. and Mishkin, M. (1982), Two cortical visual systems, in D. J. Ingle, M. A. Goodale, and R. J. W. Mansfield (eds), *Analysis of Visual Behaviour.* Cambridge, MA: MIT Press, 549–86.

Young, John Z. (1978), *Programs of the Brain.* Oxford: Oxford University Press.

Zeki, Semir (1999), *Inner Visions.* Oxford: Oxford University Press.

5a Blindness

Anstis, Stuart (1967), Visual adaptation to gradual change of intensity. *Science* 155: 710–12.

—— (1979), Interactions between simultaneous contrast and adaptation to gradual changes of luminance. *Perception* 8: 487–95.

Gregory, R. L. (1961), The brain as an engineering problem, in W. H. Thorpe and O. L. Zangwill (eds), *Current Problems in Animal Behaviour.* London: Methuen.

—— and Wallace, G. (1963), *Recovery from Early Blindness,* Monograph 2: Society of Experimental Psychology. Cambridge: Heffers.

Hick, William (1952), Experiments on the rate of gain of information. *Quarterly Journal of Experimental Psychology* 4: 11–26.

Hull, John M. (1991), *Touching the Rock.* Preston: Arrow.

Karnath, H.-O., Milner, D., and Vallar, G. (2002), *The Cognitive and Neural Bases of Spatial Neglect.* Oxford: Oxford University Press.

Miller, G. A. (1956), The magic number seven plus or minus two: some limits on our capacity to process information. *Psychological Review* 63: 81–97.

Robertson, Ian H. and Marshall, John C. (1980), *Unilateral Neglect: Clinical and Experimental Studies.* Hove: Lawrence Earlbaum.

Sacks, Oliver (1985), *The Man who Mistook his Wife for a Hat.* New York: Summit Books.

Shannon, Claude E. and Weaver, W. (1949), *The Mathematical Theory of Information*. Urbana, IL: University of Illinois Press.

5b Confounded Ambiguity

Fisher, Ronald (1934), *Design of Experiments and Statistical Methods*. Edinburgh: Oliver and Boyd.

Gregory R. L. and Cane, V. R. (1955), A statistical information theory of visual thresholds. *Nature* 176: 1272.

5c Flipping Ambiguity

Hill, H. and Bruce, V. (1993), Independent effects of lighting, orientation, and stereopsis on the Hollow Face illusion. *Perception* **22.8**: 887–97.

Hohwy, J., Roepstorff, A., and Friston, K. (2008), Predictive coding explains binocular rivalry: an epistemological review, *Cognition* 108: 687–701.

Rubin, E. (1921), *Visuael wahrgenommene Figuren*. Copenhagen: Gyldendalske.

Warren, R. M. and Gregory, R. L. (1958), An auditory analogue of the visual reversible figure. *American Journal of Psychology* 71: 612–13.

5d Instability

Bruce, V. and Young, A. (2000), *In the Eye of the Beholder: The Science of Face Perception*. Oxford: Oxford University Press.

Gregory R. L. (1959), A blue filter technique for detecting eye movements during the autokinetic effect. *Quarterly Journal of Experimental Psychology* 11: 113.

—— (1977), Vision with isoluminant colour contrast IA projection technique and observations. *Perception* 6.1: 13-119.

—— (1995), Brain-created visual motion: an illusion? *Proceedings of the Royal Society of London B* 260: 167–8.

Howard, I. P. and Rogers, B. J. (2002), *Seeing in Depth*, 2 vols. Oxford: Oxford University Press.

Livingstone, M. S. and Hubel, D. H. (1984), Anatomy and physiology of a colour system in the primary visual cortex. *Journal of Neuroscience* 4: 309–56.

Miller, D., Williams, D. R., Morris, G. M., and Laing, J. (1996), Images of cone receptors in the living human eye. *Visual Research* 36: 1067–79.

Ramachandran, V. S. and Gregory, R. L. (1978), Does colour provide an input to the human motion perception? *Nature* 275: 55–6.

Thompson, P. (1980), Margaret Thatcher: a new illusion. *Perception* 9.4: 483–4.

Wade, N. J. (1983), *Brewster & Wheatstone on Vision*. London: Academic Press.

Wheatstone, Sir Charles (1838), *Stereoscopic vision*. London: The Royal Institution.

5e Distortion

Boerse, J., Ashton, R., and Shaw, C. (1992), The apparent shape of after-images in an Ames Room. *Perception* 21: 262–8.

Dwyer, J., Ashton, R., and Boerse, J. (1990), Emmert's Law in the Ames Room. *Perception* 19: 35–41.

Feynman, R. P. (1985), *QED: The Strange Theory of Light and Matter*. Harmondsworth: Penguin.

Gillam, B. (1998), Illusions at century's end, in J. Hochberg (ed.), *Handbook of Perception and Cognition* (2nd edn). London: Academic Press, 95–136.

Gregory, R. L. (1963), Distortion of visual space and inappropriate constancy scaling. *Nature* 199: 678–90.

—— (1968), Perceptual illusions and brain models. *Proceedings of the Royal Society B* 171: 179–296.

—— (1980), Perceptions as hypotheses. *Philosophical Transactions of the Royal Society B* 290: 183–97.

—— (1997*a*), *Eye and Brain*, 5th edn. Oxford: Oxford University Press.

—— (1997*b*), *Mirrors in Mind*. Oxford: W. H. Freeman.

Gregory, R. L. (1999), Shaving in a mirror with Ockham's razor, *Interdisciplinary Science Reviews* 24.1 (Jan.): 45–51.

—— (2005), The Medawar Lecture 2001: Knowledge for vision: vision for knowledge. *Philosophical Transactions of the Royal Society B—Biological Sciences* 360.1458: 1231–51.

—— (2008), Emmert's Law and the moon illusion. *Spatial Vision* 21.3-5: 407–20.

—— and Harris, J. (1975), Illusion-destruction by appropriate scaling. *Perception* 4: 203–20.

—— and Heard, P. (1979), Border Locking and the Café Wall Illusion. *Perception* 8. 4: 365–80.

—— —— (1982), Luminance-induced shifts of edges and stereo depth, and 'Border Locking'. *Proceedings of the Physiological Society, Journal of Physiology* 327: 69–70.

—— —— (1983), Visual dissociations of movement, position and stereo depth: some phenomenal phenomena. *Quarterly Journal of Experimental Psychology* 35A: 217–37.

—— Wallace, J. G., and Campbell, F.W. (1959), Changes in size and shape of visual after-images observed in complete darkness during changes of position in space. *Quarterly Journal of Experimental Psychology* 11: 54–5.

Helmholtz, H. von (1866), *Handbuch der Physiologischen Optik*. English translation (1924) by J. P. C. Southall, *Treatise on Physiological Optics*. From the third German edn. (Hambeutg: Vossa). New York: Dover 1962. [Quotation from vol. III, p. 2].

Hick, W. E. (1952), The Rate of Gain of Information. *The Quarterly Journal of Experimental Psychology* 4.1: 11–26.

Holway, A. H. and Boring, E. G. (1941), Determinants of apparent visual size with distance variant. *American Journal of Psychology* 54: 21–37.

Humphry, N. K. and Morgan, M. J. (1965), Constancy and the geometrical illusion. *Nature* 208: 744–5.

Ittleson, W. H. (1968), *The Ames Demonstrations in Perception*. New York: Heffner.

—— and Kilpatrick, F. P. (1951), Experiments in Perception. *Scientific American* 185: 50–5.

Julesz, B. (1971), *Foundations of Cyclopean Perception*. Chicago: University of Chicago Press.

Lit, A. (1949), The magnitude of the Pulfrich stereo-phenomenon as a function of binocular differences of intensity at various levels of illumination. *American Journal of Psychology* 62: 159–81.

Murray, S. O., Boyaci, H., and Kersten, D. (2006), The representation of perceived angular size in the human primary visual cortex. *Nature Neuroscience* 109.3: 439–44.

Rogers, B. J. and Anstis, S. M. (1972), Intensity versus adaptation and the Pulfrich stereo phenomenon. *Vision Research* 12: 909–28.

Ross, H. and Plug, C. (2002), *The Mystery of the Moon Illusion*. Oxford: Oxford University Press.

Segall, H. H., Campbell, D. T., and Herskovits, M. J. (1966), *The Influence of Culture on Visual Perception*. Indianapolis: Bobbs-Merrill.

Smith, A. Mark (1996), Ptolemy's theory of visual perception, *Transactions of the American Philosophical Society* 86.2: 101–2.

Westheimer, G. (2007), Irradiation, border location, and the shifted-chessboard pattern, *Perception* 36: 483–94.

5f Fiction

Dennett, Daniel C. (1991), *Consciousness Explained*. Cambridge, MA: MIT Press.

Gregory R. L. (1972), Cognitive contours. *Nature* 238: 51–2.

—— (1978), Illusory contours and occluding surfaces, in S. Petry and G. E. Meyer (eds), *The Perception of Illusory Contours*. New York: Springer-Verlag, 131–42.

—— and Harris J. M. (1974), Illusory contours and stereo depth. *Perception and Psychophysics* 15.3: 411–16.

Harris, J. M. and Gregory, R. L. (1973), Fusion and rivalry of illusory contours. *Perception* 2: 225–47.

Heydt, Peterhans R. von der and Baumgartner, G. (1984), Illusory contours and cortical neuron responses. *Science* 224: 1260–1.

Hubel, D. H. and Weisel T. N. (1962), Receptive fields, binocular interaction and functional architecture in the cat's visual cortex. *Journal of Physiology* 160: 106.

Kanizsa, G. (1950), Subjective contours. *Scientific American* 235.4: 48–52.

Petry, Susan and Meyer, G. E. (1987), *The Perception of Illusory Contours*. New York: Springer-Verlag.

Ramachandran V. S. and Gregory R. L (1991), Perceptual filling in of artificially induced scotomas in human vision. *Nature* 350.6320: 699–702.

Schiller, Peter H. and Carvey, Christina E. (2005), The Hermann grid illusion revisited. *Perception* 34.11: 1375–97.

Schumann F. (1900), Beitraege zur Analyse der Gesichtswahrnehmungen. Este Abhandlung. Einige Beobachtungen uber die Zusammenfassung von Gesichtseindrue zu Einheiten. [Contribution to the analysis of visual perception. First paper: Some observations on the combination of visual impressions into units].

Woodworth, R. S. (1938), *Experimental Psychology*. New York: Holt. (Schumann figure on p. 637.)

5g Paradox

Draper, S. W. (1978), The Penrose triangle and a family of related figures. *Perception* 7.3: 283–96.

Ernst, B. (2006) *Optical Illusions*. Taschen.

Gregory, R. L. (1966), *Eye and Brain*. London: Duckworth; later editions Oxford: Oxford University Press.

Lockere, J. L. (2000) *The Magic of M. C. Escher*. New York: Harry N. Abrams.

Penrose, R. and Penrose, L. (1958), Impossible objects: a special type of illusions. *British Journal of Psychology* 49: 31.

Reutersvärd, O. (1934), *Swedish Postal Service (Postal)*.

Segall, M. H., Campbell, D. T., and Herskovitz, M. J. (1966), *The Influence of Culture on Visual Perception*. Indianapolis, IN: Bobbs-Merrill.

6 Perceptions to Consciousness

Darwin C. (1872), *Expression of the Emotions in Man and Animals*. London: John Murray.

Gregory R. L. (1980), Perceptions as hypotheses. *Philosophical Transactions of the Royal Society of London B*, 290: 181–97.

—— (1981), *Mind in Science*. London: Weidenfeld and Nicholson.

—— (1997), Knowledge in perception and illusion. *Philosophical Transactions of the Royal Society of London B*, 352.1: 121–8.

—— (1998), The brainy mind. *British Medical Journal* 317: 1693–5.

Huxley A. (1968), *The Complete Works of Aldous Huxley*. London: Chatto and Windus.

James, W. (1890), *Principles of Psychology*. London: Macmillan.

Kosslyn, S. M., Thompson, W. I., Kim, I. J., and Alpert, N. M. (1995), Topographical representations of mental images in primary visual cortex. *Nature* 378: 496–8.

Luria, A. (1969), *The Mind of a Mnemonist: A Little Book about a Vast Memory*. New York: Cape.

Mach, E. (1959), *Analysis of Sensation*, trans. S. Waterluw. New York: Dover.

Posner, M. I., and Raichle, M. E. (1994), *Images of Mind*. New York: Freeman.

Silbersweig, D. A., Stern, E., Filth, C., Cahill, C., Holmes, A., Grootonk, S. *et al.* (1995), A functional neuroanatomy of hallucinations in schizophrenia. *Nature* 378: 176–9.

Wason, P. and Johnson-Laird, P. (1966), *Psychology of Reasoning*. London: Batsford.

Table 2. PEERIODIC TABLE OF ILLUSIONS

KINDS	CAUSES			
	Reception	Perception		Conception
	Bottom-up Signals	Side-ways Rules	Top-down Knowledge	Understanding
BLINDNESS	*Total blindness* Loss of light, or neural processing damage. Long-term blindness has no sensation—like behind one's head. *Colour blindness* From loss of colour channels, or spectral shift of cones. 'Cross-talk' between channels.	*Nonsensical perception* **Inappropriate rules** Perceptual rules are not laws of physics. They generate Perceptual Hypotheses which may be nonsense, such as paradoxes, from false knowledge or assumptions. When rules are inappropriate, illusions occur with normally functioning physiology. Then explanation must be from Rules (or misleading Knowledge) and not from the physiology, when this is working normally.	*Agnosia* **Lack of visual knowledge** So failure to recognise even familiar things. *Change-Blindness* Small irrelevant changes not seen. 'Perceptual Hypothesis' continues until checked or challenged). *Inattention-blindness* As in conjuring. *Familiarity Blindness.* Low information signals ignored as often useless.	**Ignorance** Without understanding, the world looks like a conjuring trick. But perceptual experience can be very different from conceptual understanding, and they may conflict.

	Distinguishing stimuli	*Distinguishing objects*	*Classifying objects*	*Classifying from explanations*
CONFOUNDED AMBIGUITY	Limited by neural noise, and lost with overlapping response curves. *Colour* Cone receptors need more light than the rods. Red + green yellow light looks the same as monochromatic yellow, as the R and G pigments overlap, so both are mixtures.	When their stimuli are the same, different objects must look the same. A small near, and large distant object have same image, and ellipse as a tilted circle *Ames Room* Has the same retinal image as a normal room—so must look the same. But interesting when objects, such as people, are inside it.	Different kinds of objects are often confounded when not familiar or understood. E.g. fossils, or makes of cars. Special knowledge with defined differences is important for classifying.	Classifications can be circular—as phenomena suggest explanations and explanations interpret phenomena. (Cladistics aims to avoid circularity in Evolutionary accounts by being theory-neutral).
FLIPPING AMBIGUITY	*The Sacred Disease* Neural nets are dynamic and can be physically unstable, especially when inhibition and	*Figure-ground* The most basic decision is whether there is an object present. This is seen dramatically in	*Alternative Perceptions* Perceptions flip to alternatives when the brain can't make up its mind. E.g. *Necker Cube,*	*'Collapsing' reality* Objects do not 'flip' to other objects—except in quantum physics. Measurements or

(*Continued*)

Table 2. (Continued)

KINDS	CAUSES			
	Reception	Perception		Conception
	Bottom-up Signals	Side-ways Rules	Top-down Knowledge	Understanding
	negative feedback fail, as in migraine.	flipping figure-ground ambiguity, when the brain cannot make up its mind Object recognition starts from general rules, such as the Gestalt Laws, but when they are inadequate or conflicting, figure-ground is unstable.	*Duck-Rabbit.* **Hollow Face** Probabilities normally give stability, but can mislead. (*Hollow face* looks convex.) **Stereoscopic vision** Resolves ambiguities of distance.	perceptions are supposed to 'collapse' many possibilities into particular realities. This creation of reality by perception has been ascribed to consciousness, but this is totally mysterious.
INSTABILITY	*Jazzing figures* Op. Art. McKay Rays' (Repeated lines stimulate on-off cells with eye tremor). *Retinal rivalry* Shimmering of polished metal. *Shifting contours*	*Grouping* Random dot patterns group and regroup, Gestalt Rules: closure, contiguity, common fate etc.—from Bayesian probabilities. *Glass Effect* Random dot pattern	*Constancy Scaling* *The world generally looks stable in spite of observer motion.* Constancies partially compensate motion; but when inappropriate, Constancy Scaling generates illusions—of	**Conceiving Objects** Perception constructs object-hypotheses in real time; but conceptions are generally timeless. Both are unstable with conflicting or inadequate data.

		At isoluminance Ouchi illusion (Lack of 'border-locking'?)	superimposed on itself and slightly displaced shows lines, or if rotated, circles.	motion, size and shape distortions and many more.
DISTORTION	**Signal distortions** Many visual illusions are due to signal errors, such as cross-talk and lateral inhibition. *After-effects* *Of continuous motion, distortions from tilt, curvature, spatial frequency, colour, etc.* After-effects may serve to re-calibrate the senses, but can be wrong.	**Cognitive distortions** "Geometrical or 'perspective' distortions: Müller-Lyer; Ponzo; Hering; Poggendorff; Horizontal-Vertical; Harvest Moon, etc. On the Misapplied Scaling theory, Depth cues miss-set size-scaling—features signalled as more a distant being expanded. Scaling can also be set 'downwards'.	**Anticipation** Prediction is essential for cognitive perception—but can mislead *Size-weight illusion.* Smaller objects feel heavier than larger objects of the same scale weight. False expectation, as larger objects are usually heavier—setting too much muscle power when actually the same.	**Reference truths** An object cannot itself be distorted, but may differ from accepted references. Thus a ruler is bent, or too long or too short, by reference to some other ruler, accepted as 'true'. Reference to non-illusions is essential for measuring illusions; though illusions and errors can show up as internal inconsistencies.
FICTION	**Spurious signals** After-images appear as objects that would give the same images, in	**Grouping** Random dots group into object-like shapes, with the Gestalt Laws—	**Phantasms** *Faces-in-the-fire; man-in-the-moon; inkblots.* These show the creative	**Indirectly related to reality** Perceptions and Conceptions are at best indirectly related to

(Continued)

Table 2. (Continued)

KINDS	CAUSES			
	Reception		Perception	Conception
	Bottom-up Signals	Side-ways Rules	Top-down Knowledge	Understanding
	external space. *Phi movement* Alternating separated lights appear as a single moving light, by stimulating normal movement systems, which are tolerant of gaps.	similarity, common fates, etc. *Ghosts* Object-shaped gaps can be evidence of nearer occluding objects, creating fictional objects such as the Kanizsa Triangle.	dynamics of perception, when alternative hypotheses are evoked. As perception is dynamic, perceptions can break free from stimulus control, with a life of their own.	reality, and being dynamic constructions can easily take off as fiction.
PARADOX	*Conflicting signals* Neural channels signal various object properties and states of play. Parallel channels can disagree, as when some	*Impossible objects* The Impossible Triangle can exist yet from certain positions it appears impossible. Perceptual Hypotheses	*Knowledge conflicts* *Magritte's painting of the back of a man's head— the back of the head appearing in the mirror instead of his face.*	*Mind and physics* Although the brain is a physical system perceptions and conceptions are not limited by physics;

are adapted differently. Then perceptions may be impossible. The *Spiral after-effect* expands or shrinks, yet without changing size.	generated from false assumptions can be paradoxical. The sides of the Impossible Triangle touch optically at the corners, though some are separated in depth. The false assumption of touching physically generates the paradox.	This disturbs, as it goes counter to one's implicit visual knowledge of reflections. Conflicts of signals with failed predictions, are key to correcting present and evoking new perceptions.	making it possible to see and imagine impossibilities, even to experiencing logical paradoxes. Much the same holds for computer software also not limited by physical laws, and may be paradoxical.

INDEX